D1591139

42 Rules of Product Management

Learn the Rules of Product Management from Leading Experts from Around the World

**By Brian Lawley
and Greg Cohen**

/UPER/taR

E-mail: info@superstarpress.com
20660 Stevens Creek Blvd., Suite 210
Cupertino, CA 95014

Copyright © 2010 by Brian Lawley and Greg Cohen

All rights reserved. No part of this book shall be reproduced, stored in a retrieval system, or transmitted by any means electronic, mechanical, photocopying, recording, or otherwise without written permission from the publisher.

Published by Super Star Press™, a Happy About® imprint
20660 Stevens Creek Blvd., Suite 210, Cupertino, CA 95014
http://42rules.com

First Printing: October 2010
Second Printing: November 2010
Paperback ISBN: 978-1-60773-086-6 (1-60773-086-3)
eBook ISBN: 978-1-60773-087-3 (1-60773-087-1)
Place of Publication: Silicon Valley, California, USA
Library of Congress Number: 2010938034

Trademarks

All terms mentioned in this book that are known to be trademarks or service marks have been appropriately capitalized. Neither Happy About®, nor any of its imprints, can attest to the accuracy of this information. Use of a term in this book should not be regarded as affecting the validity of any trademark or service mark.

Warning and Disclaimer

Every effort has been made to make this book as complete and as accurate as possible. The information provided is on an "as is" basis. The author(s), publisher, and their agents assume no responsibility for errors or omissions. Nor do they assume liability or responsibility to any person or entity with respect to any loss or damages arising from the use of information contained herein.

Dedication

This book is dedicated to all of the product managers who are passionate about bringing great new products to market.

Acknowledgments

We would like to thank the all star team of product management experts worldwide who contributed their time and wisdom to this project. Without them this book would not be possible. By sharing your knowledge and wisdom, you have helped to further the profession of product management.

A special thanks to the 280 Group team and to Jillian McLaughlin for project managing the book. We also want to thank our editor Laura Lowell, our production manager Liz Tadman, and our copy editor Deneene Bell.

Lastly, we would like to express our appreciation to our families for their support and patience during the creation of this book.

Contents

Contents

Back when I started my career as a product manager, things were quite different than they are today. There were no books or training courses. There were no product management associations, blogs, or newsletters. Email was just in its infancy, and the World Wide Web was merely an experiment being conducted by a small group of elite technologists. The only way that you learned how to be a great product manager was by trial and (often painful) error. Occasionally, if you were lucky, you would have a manager who could teach you the subtleties and mentor you (I had several and they made a huge difference in my career).

My, how things have changed. There are all kinds of resources available to help you learn the profession of product management. Product management has grown up; companies are recognizing what a key role it plays in the success or failure of their products and their overall results. And along with all of this, there are many product management experts who have emerged that are enthusiastic about sharing what they have learned about the profession.

The goal of this book is to expose you to the wisdom and knowledge from a group of the world's leading product management experts. Among the contributors, there are leading authors, professors, CEOs and vice presidents, bloggers, consultants, trainers, and even a few salespeople and engineers. In total, there are over five centuries of collected wisdom represented here.

To put the book together, we reached out to a large number of people throughout the world. (If you were not included, please don't be offended. Email us and let us know so we can include you in future projects like this.) The rules were submitted over a two-month period. Each rule stands on its own, and they are not in any particular order in the book.

NOTE: We received more rules than we were able to publish. We will be posting these on our Product Management 2.0 Blog at: http://280group.com/blog and in our newsletter, so make sure you sign up.

It is our sincere hope that the rules in this book will help make your product management career more enjoyable and more successful. And equally important, we hope that it will lead to you shipping products that your customers love and that are wildly successful and highly profitable.

Brian Lawley
CEO and Founder, 280 Group
October 2010

1

Rules Are Meant to Be Broken

Greg Cohen, Senior
Principal Consultant, 280 Group

"Learn the rules so you know how to break them properly."
– Dalai Lama

The best product managers I have known are independent people who are passionate about their products and have deep conviction about how to make them succeed. Sometimes this means bending the rules, disregarding the advice of management, and ignoring conventional wisdom. This is important for progress. We must always look at things in new ways. For often, true innovation requires that we challenge the status quo in the creation of new products that deliver significantly more value to the customer than existing alternatives. If we are fortunate, have done our homework, and are right in our conviction, we can even create an entirely new market. Some successful examples of rule breakers include:

Henry Ford creating affordable automobiles: In 1908, Henry Ford produced an automobile that was differentiated in one characteristic—it was the first "affordable" automobile. The price continued to drop each year and within ten years, 50 percent of cars in the United States were Ford Model Ts.[i]

Frederick Smith of FedEx with guaranteed overnight delivery of goods: Fred Smith launched his overnight delivery service in April 1973 with a twenty-five-city network. On its first day, the company delivered 186 packages. Smith worked hard to grow the company's volume and network, but also had to contend with a postal monopoly that prevented FedEx from delivering packages and ill-suited airline regulations that first restricted the company to flying only small jets.[ii] The company struggled to have enough cash to survive during these early years. Federal Express became profitable in 1975 and was finally allowed to fly large jets in 1977 when air cargo was deregulated. Today FedEx is a household brand with worldwide operations and its fleet travels nearly five hundred thousand miles per day.[iii]

Masura Ibuka of Sony with the transistor radio: Although not the inventor of the transistor radio, Masura Ibuka saw its potential and seized upon the opportunity to license the technology from AT&T when they made it available in 1952. Ibuka and partner Akio Morita convinced Japan's Ministry of International Trade and Industry (MITI) to finance the $25,000 licensing fee and then went to work creating the first "pocket" radio under the Sony brand.[iv] Sony repeated a similar feat of miniaturization in 1978 when it introduced its Walkman line of portable cassette players.[v]

Each of the individuals above knew that the path to success would not be achieved by following the rules. Each also dealt with many setbacks. Ford did not succeed until his third company. His first company, Detroit Automobile Company, failed, and he left his second, which later became Cadillac, due to a disagreement with investors. The first Model T cars only came in black. Similarly with Sony, Ibuka's first two radios were not commercially successful. His third attempt still had inferior sound quality to the tube radios of the day. Fred Smith overcame the rules of commerce including airline regulation and the US Postal Service's monopoly. What carried all three visionaries through these challenging times was the strength of their convictions and their willingness to break rules in pursuit of customer value.

Thus, believing in yourself is key and creating customer value is paramount. These two things are all that really matter. You must trust in yourself to have the strength necessary to deal with the adversity and setbacks that sit between product failure and product success. Further, only by creating customer value do we ensure the long-term viability of our respective companies. Generating profits and shareholder value are secondary. These are outcomes of delivering a product to the market that customers find valuable and better than the alternatives. Each of the visionaries above understood this.

Use this book as a guide on your journey. The 42 rules contain much hard-earned wisdom. But always remember, *rules are meant to be broken.*

2

Work on Products You Are Passionate About

Brian Lawley,
CEO and Founder, 280 Group

The one common factor that I have noticed about the best product managers is that they choose to work on products that they are very passionate about.

Let's face it, product management can be a tough job. We often have a lot of responsibility yet little formal authority. There are multiple groups of stakeholders (customers, management, salespeople, support, etc.) who all have ideas and demands that they wish to see included in our products, which means we end up having to say "no" often. In some cases, we work in engineering-driven companies, which creates a culture where it is difficult to influence and have a big impact on the products we manage.

I also believe that product management can also be the most interesting job in the world. Being able to set product strategy, lead your team to create products that your customers love, and be responsible for the overall success of a product can be exhilarating.

The one common factor that I have noticed about the best product managers is that they choose to work on products that they are very passionate about. It could be a passion for the technology, for solving a hard customer problem, or for changing the way customers work or play. Or it could be a passion for capturing a market and implementing a winning strategy. But, nonetheless, there is passion for what they are doing.

I have managed many different products in my career. In my experience, the times when I enjoyed my job the most were when I was working on something that I had tremendous passion for. At Apple, I was the product manager for the Macintosh Human Interface—though it was an incredibly difficult job, I loved what I was doing. At Symantec,

I was in charge of C++ and Java development tools. Although the product didn't excite me, the prospect of capturing the market when Java first appeared did excite me, and we managed to do just that.

So why is passion so important? Even in the best of product management jobs there are always going to be some very difficult challenges. If you are working on something that you don't care deeply about you simply won't have the tenacity and persistence to do what needs to be done in order for the product to succeed. This drive to succeed has to come from within. No one can "command" you to be passionate about your product. I have seen many product managers fall into the trap of working on things they really don't care about and ultimately they end up hurting their careers and chances for advancement.

The other reason that passion is so important is that it is infectious. If your team sees that you are excited about and committed to what you are doing, it will carry over to them. Your salespeople will be more excited about selling your products. The engineers will be more excited about what they are building. And your company will know that your products are important and are going to succeed.

Life is short. Work on something that you really care about. If you aren't doing this right now, make a commitment to make a change. Either make the change or else find some aspect about the products you are managing that can get you excited. Perhaps you can set a market share or revenue goal and get the corresponding strategy and tactics into place to see if you can make it happen. Or perhaps in parallel with your day-to-day work you can identify some unmet customer needs and help your company bring a brand new product to market. Whatever you do, don't waste your life by working on something you don't care about deeply.

3 Beware the "Requirements Death Spiral"

Greg Cohen, Senior Principal Consultant, 280 Group

Thus, the spiral begins. With each subsequent release, the product manager demands ever more detailed time estimates.... Development, in turn, demands ever more detailed requirements.

A pattern I've observed in multiple companies over the years is product managers defining features and the corresponding implementation in excruciating detail in their requirements documentation. When I see this, I know the company went into the "requirements death spiral." The story of each company is always remarkably similar.

It starts off simply enough and with the best intentions: A product manager provides some high level requirements to their development team and asks for an estimate to do the work. When the estimate is longer than the time available, the product manager asks the team if they could try to make it happen by the deadline and assures them that the product is really very straightforward and there are no hidden surprises. Because the team wants to be accommodating, it agrees.

As the development progresses, new requirements are added as more is learned, but the team is told the release date cannot move, sections of the requirements are misunderstood, the resultant solution does not match the product manager's or customer's expectations, rework is needed, and the schedule inevitably slips. Feeling powerless, the product manager points the finger at engineering for missing the date and getting the product wrong. Being blamed after having worked overtime and with heroic efforts, engineering points the finger right back at the product manager for not being clear on what he wanted and frequently changing his mind.

For the next release, the product manager—a little wiser now—asks the development lead to sign off on the requirements. This way the engineering team will somehow think it is legally bound to the terms of the requirements document. Product management also presses the engineering team to ensure the delivery date will be met. Having been burned once—and also a little wiser—the engineering manager starts to pad the dates and says that he cannot commit to anything sooner without more detailed requirements. This, of course, does not fix the problem.

Thus, the spiral begins. With each subsequent release, the product manager demands ever more detailed time estimates from development. Development, in turn, demands ever more detailed requirements from the product manager. Without even realizing it, the product manager begins to specify the solution (rather than needs) and the development team, not wanting to be blamed for any mishaps, starts to build exactly what is written without ever questioning it. Worst of all, the customer is disappointed and the product meets with only limited success in the marketplace.

The destructive feedback loop that sets up the requirements death spiral is a fascinating phenomenon because both sides want to create a winning product and start with the best of intentions. Further, both sides are behaving completely rationally within the scope of their area (i.e., product management or engineering). Only when viewed from the perspective of delivering value to the customer and creating value for the company are product management's and engineering's actions so clearly counterproductive.

It is product management's responsibility to identify customer problems worth solving. It is engineering's role to identify technical solutions to those problems. Together both sides must collaborate to create the optimal design that will solve the problem for the customer and delight them in its use.

Ultimately, the product manager is accountable for the product's success. Product managers, therefore, must be vigilant to avoid entering the death spiral. The easiest way to do this is to focus on the problem space and encourage engineering to apply their creative energies to the solution space. Product management and engineering are on the same team and share the same objective of creating value for the customer. The product manager's actions must reflect this truth.

Think Like an Entrepreneur

Linda Gorchels, Director of Executive Marketing
Education, Wisconsin School of Business

At its most basic level, to think like a product manager requires thinking like an entrepreneur.

One of the expectations I received from a product manager during a recent corporate training session was to *learn how to think like a product manager.* While there are many perspectives and buzzwords that could be thrown at this objective, at its most basic level, to think like a product manager requires thinking like an entrepreneur.

Let's expand on that a bit. While people may argue that entrepreneurs have more control over everything than do product managers, the reality is just the opposite. It is the rare entrepreneur who is independently wealthy with easy access to materials, operations, and labor. Most entrepreneurs have a vision for a product or service they are passionate about, but have to find the resources to actualize the vision. They must craft business plans to solicit money from venture capitalists or banks. That's not unlike the challenges product managers face in developing business cases for new products. The business case is essentially a proposal for an investment of time and resources from the firm. In fact, some firms expect product managers to treat the management team sort of as angel investors who must be convinced of the future value of the product concept being proposed.

After receiving guarantees of funding, entrepreneurs may need to source materials or locate contract manufacturers. They must work carefully with third parties they don't directly manage to accomplish the design, development, and commercialization of their envisioned products or services. Similarly, product managers must constantly accomplish their goals through organizational functions over which they have no direct authority. They must use their skills of persuasion and diplomacy to make things happen.

Entrepreneurs often need to work with independent sales representatives or channels to reach the intended market. To help these groups function more effectively, entrepreneurs must provide not just product knowledge but also an understanding of the target markets and the best approach to reach these markets. That's akin to the challenge product managers face when training and motivating the sales force. There is a strong need to empathize with the needs of salespeople to advance the sales process.

The common link between the entrepreneurial business plan and the product manager business case is clarity of customer need. Strong entrepreneurs and strong product managers know the profile, needs, emotions, and purchase drivers of their customers. They don't think exclusively in terms of product features/benefits, but rather how these features/benefits align with customer goals better than competing offerings. They have a strong command of marketing and customer-focused competencies.

Entrepreneurs share several common traits that influence the way they think. Entrepreneurs embody traits of risk-taking, passion, focus, product/customer knowledge, and tolerance for failure. Strong product managers share these traits (or elements of these traits), which influence their thoughts and decision-making processes.

Let's carry this analogy one step further. Successful entrepreneurs can grow successful companies. (As an aside, serial entrepreneurs start *several* companies. Our focus here is NOT on serial entrepreneurs but rather those more focused on a single economic endeavor.) As their companies grow, the passion, focus, and connectedness with the product/customer becomes diffused. That's where product managers come in. Product managers can restore the passion, focus, and connectedness with the product/customer for their areas of responsibility.

So the bottom line is: to think like a product manager requires thinking like an entrepreneur.

Learn to Say "No" to Customers

Ivan Chalif, Blogger, The Productologist

Saying "no" lets product managers focus on delivering superior products rather than ones that are merely sufficient.

Product managers talk and listen to many stakeholders, because they want to understand the needs and desires of the market. An important part of that process is sharing, especially the strategic product road map. Sharing this information does two things:

1. It lets the customer know that you are willing to let information flow both ways. This helps them share more specific details (the kind product managers **really** need) and not feel like they are providing information for free.

2. Sharing also lets them see the future plans for the product and how their future plans fit with what has been mapped out.

While there are certainly benefits to sharing the road map with customers (and even sometimes prospects), it comes with drawbacks, too. Every customer has needs that are specific to their business. They frequently look to the product manager (and the product road map) to help them resolve those needs.

In many cases, that information is valuable in helping the product manager address the needs of an industry or vertical market, or even a type of user. Unfortunately, it can also lead to adding features to the product that serve only a few users. These choices are sometimes unavoidable, but, over time, they can lead to bloat, misdirection, and mediocrity of the product.

As a result of reviewing the road map and **not** seeing what they want on it, or in the time frame that they want it, customers make requests to raise the priority of a particular feature or to add a new capability to the product that was not being considered. This is where "no" comes into play for product management (see Rule 2 by Brian Lawley). Saying "no" lets product managers focus on delivering superior products, rather than ones that are merely sufficient.

Let me use the following to illustrate the value of saying "no." This is a real experience I had with a customer who repeatedly requested a feature that was very low on the priority list. No other customer (or prospect) had asked for anything similar, so it remained low on the list because it didn't align well with where we were planning to take the product.

Every conversation I had with the customer team included a question about when they would get the feature that they had been asking for so long. Early on, I would provide a response that is common amongst product managers: "We have captured the requirement for your requested feature, but it is not assigned to the next release." While this settled the discussion for the moment, it only delayed revisiting it the next time there was a release announcement.

Ultimately, I drew a line in the sand and told the customer that even though the feature was important to their business, I did not see that it would ever be in the product. Despite the customer team initially being quite upset and frustrated with my response, and getting a call from their CEO about her disappointment about the state of the product and its ability to meet their needs, telling them "no" was the right decision for them and the product.

I spoke with the customer team again several months later with a decidedly friendlier outcome. They told me that because I had told them that they wouldn't get the feature (rather than the feature being delayed), they had decided to invest in building the capabilities they needed in-house and were very happy with the results. And they were happier with my product too.

They had the feature they wanted, exactly how they wanted it, and within the time frame that they wanted. And all of this was made possible because of the power of "no."

6

Product Management Is Inherently Political

Rich Mironov, Author,
The Art of Product Management

Allocating scarce resources always leaves some people dissatisfied and drives them to escalate complaints or question the decision-making process.

Product managers tend to have very rational, process-driven views of the world. We'd like to believe that our various stakeholders are thoughtful, unemotional, and willing to compromise and put the company's overall strategic interest ahead of departmental politics and personal rewards. Of course, that's not how it is in the real world.

One of our primary jobs as product managers is to prioritize what gets done (and the many things that therefore *won't* get done soon.) Unavoidably, most of our internal customers will be unhappy with some of our choices. And that's regardless of how well we've applied "internal ROI" and other quantitative approaches to creating the best road map. MRDs are only the starting point in an ongoing lobbying campaign for product improvements. In other words, product managers will always have to manage the emotional world of people and internal politics.

Setting the Stage

You've collected a nearly infinite list of possible improvements, advances, new features, and architectural repairs. Your goal is to build one orderly list of items, review them with engineering for size and suitability, and then issue a definitive road map or requirements document (MRD or PRD) that formally declares what will be built. Being analytical and a bit compulsive, you think of this as the *end* of a long process, after which Engineering will leap into action.

You've had to make choices from a dissimilar list of potential projects:

- **Broad feature improvements** as demanded by the market, reviews, user groups, and your keen sense of what customers want
- **Internal architectural changes** that will be invisible to customers but are needed for improved quality or longer-term goals
- **Customer specials** for specific big accounts, likely to be of limited use to others
- **Bug fixes and cleanup** that reduce technical debt
- **High-profile product bets** on emerging market needs or new technologies

Trade-offs within each group are easy, but across groups are nearly impossible. Part of your job is to balance these different categories so that your next release meets a few needs from each group.

Ultimately, an MRD is the culmination of intense negotiations with all parties (engineering, marketing, sales, customers). It represents a compromise based on your best judgment and the facts on hand. Ideally, you've also made each constituent group feel valued/respected/listened to. After emailing the final MRD to all groups, your team takes you out for a well-deserved celebration. This *feels* like a milestone.

Nearly immediately, though, two kinds of problems arise. One is caused by actual changes in the world: shifting customer needs, market trends, product experience, and general evolution. The second is lobbying from the sales teams and internal groups that did not get what they wanted. By making hard choices about which features are in your next release, you've had to postpone other legitimate requests.

Political Issues Require Political Solutions

Allocating scarce resources always leaves some people dissatisfied, and drives them to escalate complaints or question the decision-making process. This is certainly true of product plans, which prioritize Engineering's projects and schedules. You can call this "politics" if you like, or "group decision-making," or any handy phrase from the MBA Organizational Behavior handbook. Regardless of the label, even the perfect MRD will leave some of your constituents unhappy. To keep the process moving forward, you need political support for the decision process and your final choices.

Generally, this involves pre-negotiation with executives in Sales, Engineering, Marketing and perhaps Finance or Manufacturing. Helping them understand your process—and how their teams will get some of the things that they need—is one way to get ahead of escalations and second-guessing.

Product managers are paid to make decisions that have an impact on the broader organization. This makes us part of the internal political process. Rather than ignore this reality, we need to understand how decisions are made and remade and work within the system.

7 There Is a Fine Line between Knowing It All and Being a Know-It-All

Alyssa Dver, CEO, Mint Green Marketing

Refrain from being the know-it-all— instead be someone that all know they can follow, learn from, and ultimately trust to lead the product toward success.

We become product managers for a variety of reasons, but our common characteristics are that we are smart, we like to be the center of attention, and, well, we feel compelled to expose those things in what we optimistically cloak as evangelism.

Product managers need to lead teams that do not report to them; they need to be decisive in the absence of perfect information, and they need to educate others about often unrelated products. Product managers also need to play judge when there are other conflicting opinions, and they need to defend their product decisions and plans despite internal and/or external argument. However, product managers also need to listen intently to input from a variety of, sometimes ignorant, stakeholders and put their own opinions aside to really hear the voices of the customers, and then some. They need to accept product failure as their own fault and yet pass on congratulations when there is success to the entire product team.

As such, product managers must check their egos at the proverbial door. Few things deteriorate a product manager's credibility and earned respect from others than a product manager who tries to explain something he/she does not understand. An engineer or other technical individual will find insult when the PM tries to overstep the line between requirements and specification, between the "why we built it" versus "how we built it." And while the product manager may ultimately be responsible for the product baby, a senior manager may pull ownership rank much like birth parents appear to claim credit and affection only once the product is successfully grown.

No, product management isn't typically a thankful position, but it is ultimately one of honor. And with that honor comes great responsibility to be a clear communicator and an understated but effective leader. Knowing how to manage your own passion while remaining committed, knowing enough about the product but, more importantly, knowing how to manage the product team and process, and, in the end, being smart enough to pick the right battles where you neither have be to defensive nor offensive in your position...well, that is the mark of a truly successful product manager.

So before you rush into a meeting filled with vim, vigor, and veracity, think about how great leaders would handle conflict and challenge. Garner intellectual and data-backed knowledge to be better prepared than a bulldozing project manager that takes no prisoners but leaves utter doubt about who is really is in command. If Martin Luther King, Nelson Mandela, or Mahatma Gandhi were product managers, they would gain consensus and collaboration using their charm and by setting their own examples. Challenge yourself to be someone worth following instead of leading with a big product management stick—after all, not many of us have the public track record of Steve Jobs or Bill Gates. Refrain from being the know-it-all—instead be someone that all know they can follow, learn from, and ultimately trust to lead the product toward success.

8 Market Research Must Be Actionable

**Luke Hohman, Founder and CEO,
The Innovation Games® Company**

Good market research answers one or more questions that help you understand your customers...in such a way that you can take confident action towards your goals.

The plethora of market research methods, and the consultants and market research firms that promote their favorite method, makes it far too easy for product management and marketing professionals to lose sight of the single most important goal in good market research: good market research is actionable.

Good market research answers one or more questions that help you understand your customers, your competitive marketplace, your competitors, and even yourself in such a way that you can take confident action towards your goals. Ultimately, effective market research is:

- Systematic—planned, well-organized, with a goal and a method
- Objective—minimal researcher or method bias
- Focused—on specific questions
- Actionable—the results obtained enable you to take action

The first letter from each of these words forms the acronym SOFA, and, like a comfortable sofa, effective market research provides a comfortable position for taking action.

Also realize you don't need a big budget to conduct market research. In fact, you **don't** need a lot of things to do great market research. You don't need:

- a big budget
- a marketing degree from a prestigious university
- a degree in statistics
- the perfect respondent

Oh, sure, these things can help, and, yes, of course, in certain specialized circumstances, they may be required. But for the vast majority of product managers and product marketing professionals, you don't need a lot of what people think you need to do great market research.

What you **do** need to conduct great market research is:

*   a commitment to understanding your customers
*   the willingness to accept results that do not match your preconceived ideas
*   specific questions, a method appropriate to getting the answers, and the readiness to act

Whoa. That's a pretty small list. Too small for your taste? You are welcome to add some of your own requirements as to what you think you need. But be careful: Requirements are like chili powder. A little goes a long way, and too much spoils the pot.

So stop stressing about whether or not you should be starting with primary market research or secondary market research. Stop thinking that the only way to make your case is through statistical significance. And stop selecting your method based on the tools you know, the tools your boss likes, or the software licenses your company has signed with a market research vendor.

Start instead by getting on the SOFA of market research. Ask yourself: What are my questions? What will I do with the answers? Once you're clear, or at least as clear as you can get, find the market research approach that will help you get the answers. If that requires a statistically significant, multi-month, ask-my-boss-for-more-budget conjoint analysis, then by all means make your case for more budget. If it means using collaborative play such as Innovation Games® with your customers, then do that. And if it means something else entirely, well, that's just fine too. The important thing is to start actually **listening** to your customers (in any of the many wonderful ways you can).

9

The Two-Week Rule

Marty Cagan, Author, *Inspired*

Never go more than two weeks without putting your product ideas in front of real users and customers.

You've worked hard, you've generated a compelling business case, you've spent time designing and writing specs, you've solicited the input from a number of customers and stakeholders, you've answered countless questions from the developers, and you finally launch. Yet the product fails. It's either something that the customers just didn't want once they saw it, or they couldn't figure out how to use it, or it would have taken so long to build that you were forced to gut it just to get it shipped in a reasonable time frame.

It may have failed due to any number of issues: your customers didn't really want what they thought they wanted; you didn't have capable designers; you were confusing yourself with your customer; you didn't get engineering's input until it was too late; or one hundred other reasons.

But all of these would have been preventable if you had just been able to get the product concept in front of real users early enough in the process to have determined if the product was destined to succeed or fail.

A lot of people think the only way to get this feedback is to design it, build it, launch it, and then see what happens. There are a few cases where that's true, but it's rare. For the most part, especially for Web products, we can, in fact, get the feedback we need in the time frame we need it, if we focus on the right activities—prototyping and testing that prototype on real users—rather than spending our time creating business cases, gathering requirements, and writing specs.

But another less obvious dynamic happens when we wait too long to get feedback from real users and customers: we get too attached to our own ideas.

Many product managers hold off for months before they get any real validation of the ideas with the people that matter. And every day that goes by the product team gets increasingly deeper and more entangled with their original idea to the point that now they're either too scared to show it to customers for fear of having to start over, or they are so confident that it will be great that they think they can just skip to development, or they've got developers screaming at them just to give them something to build.

So for those people that believe in the principle that they need to validate their product ideas with real users, but are unsure of how "baked" the idea needs to be, I offer this very explicit rule—never go more than two weeks without putting your product ideas in front of real users and customers.

Does this mean your ideas won't be fully fleshed out yet? Yes, and good.

Does this mean that customers might not like your ideas? Yes, and good.

Remember, it's all about failing fast.

You can and should continue to refine your product ideas—it's not like you have two weeks to define every last pixel. But you must get out of the office and put your ideas in front of real users while you still have time to adapt.

At Facebook they like the mantra, "Don't fall in love," as a way to ensure that the product team doesn't get so enamored of their own ideas that they ignore or rationalize the feedback from the people that matter.

Steve Blank has a great line about this: "In a startup, no facts exist inside the building, only opinions." I believe strongly that the most important thing that a product manager must do is put his ideas in front of real users and watch their responses.

Remember that your job as a product manager is to define a successful product and have evidence that the product will be successful, not just your opinion. And you won't find that evidence inside your building.

10 Market Needs, Not Individual Requests

Jeff Lash, Blogger,
How to Be a Good Product Manager

Good product managers listen to their customers, but more importantly they listen to the market.

Product management seems to start out so easily—you identify a need for a product, you build it, and you start getting customers. Then things get complicated. Current customers start asking for changes to existing features. Sales starts creating a list of "must haves" for the product that will help them close that elusive next deal. Competitors start popping up, copying your product but also adding new features that threaten to steal your user base. Executives come up with "brilliant" ideas that they want included in the next release.

On an almost daily basis, product managers face requests for new features and product changes. Attempting to address or even track all of them is an uphill battle that no product manager can hope to win.

We are conditioned by pithy phrases like, "The customer is always right," and mantras like, "customer focused," to assume that everything a customer requests is reasonable, and that not reacting to it is a capital offense. Unfortunately, this mentality just compounds the problem.

Product managers succeed when they stop responding to specific demands from individual customers and start listening to the market as a whole.

Current customers are an incredibly important constituency—though not the only one. It's very easy to find out what they like and dislike—in fact, it's sometimes hard to avoid hearing what they think! The only problem is that they're already your customers, and, undoubtedly, you have more potential customers than you have current customers. How are you going to grow revenue by just serving your existing base? How are you going to expand into new markets when you're not focusing on what those customers need?

As a product manager, I've always learned a lot **more** about what can be done to improve my product by talking to people who are **not buying** it, and people who are buying it and then **not using** it. When you ask a current customer what they don't like about your product, they'll likely point to things they don't like which they think should be added or fixed—things they discovered after purchasing it and which they feel should be improved "for free." Talk to a competitor's customer, however, and they'll tell you why they didn't buy your product, and what you would have to do to your product to make it worth purchasing. Talk to a customer in a totally new market segment, and they'll tell you what their problems are and how much they'd pay to have them resolved. That's practically money in the bank!

When you start looking at the market as a whole, you start identifying opportunities to really identify solutions that will provide value. Rather than just making an improvement that will address a specific pain point for a few customers, you start to find opportunities to grow your business and make you relevant to a much bigger potential customer base.

Current users will tell you where their pain points are today, though they won't tell you where their pain points will be three years from now. They can't tell you about the problems facing another industry; they won't be able to tell you about what upcoming technology innovations will change their operations; and they don't know why people aren't buying from you. Requests from your existing customer base are not to be ignored, especially when you are dependent on them for ongoing revenue (e.g., subscription based products, software-as-a-service). However, evaluate them in the bigger context of the market as a whole.

11

No Surprises

Jim Reekes, Senior
Principal Consultant, 280 Group

The only surprise a product manager should give anyone is, "Hey, we blew away our forecast!" The type of surprise you never want is, "WTF!?"

Consider your Market Requirements Document (MRD). It can be filled with surprises, and I mean that in a bad way. Before you hand it to your engineering group, talk to them about it. Before writing your ideas down, share them in person. Tell the team what (and how) you're thinking. Ask them what format works best. Do they prefer story mode or tables with rows of categories, priorities, sources, etc.? Do they understand the difference between "shall" and "should," or my preference of "must" and "may?"

I mention that last one because I was once surprised when half way into the development cycle engineering decided not to implement a requirement I had listed as a "shall." When I asked how could they drop an absolute requirement, they argued with me about—I'm not kidding—the definition of "shall." WTF? I reminded them when Moses came down from the mountain with those Ten Commandments they were not nice-to-haves—they were absolutes written as "You shall."

As you are writing the MRD, talk through the ideas informally with them, clarifying the customer's need and why it is important. If you deliver a document loaded with surprises, they will not take ownership of it and may not support your efforts (or worse, may simply ignore it). Even before submitting your first draft of the MRD, all of your readers should (no, make that "shall") have heard of its contents from you firsthand. This goes for all of your stakeholders (customers, salespeople, support, engineering, marketing, management, etc.)

Be transparent with everyone on how you gather and prioritize require-ments. Explain your method of prioritization. Many times people just want to know their ideas are being considered. If you reassure them and show them that you have a logical way of capturing and prioritizing, they will be much more accepting if their feature doesn't make in.

When attending or running meetings that include a potential bad surprise, especially with people who have strong opinions, always float those ideas by them beforehand. Phrase the idea in the form of a question and ask what they think (engineers love to think). They'll likely be so engaged with explaining everything down to the minutiae that they'll not realize you're pandering to their intellect. It's like Judo. They want to look smart (and make you feel dumb). The idea of no surprises also includes avoiding the risk of blindsiding the person in a public setting with something that might be a sensitive. If you surprise them in a meeting this way, there's no pre-dicting what could happen. You don't want this to happen.

I shouldn't have to mention this, but it happens way too many times not to highlight it. The biggest source of surprises (and abuse) is email. Email is a great tool, but the tone and content can easily be misinterpreted. It is always better to talk live with a person to avoid misunderstandings.

Lastly, and most importantly, don't surprise anyone about what your role actually is. This is usually a big surprise and a bad one. There's a long list of responsibilities for a product manager, and few people understand them. They probably think they own some of that list. Be clear on what you do and don't do with everyone, and evangelize this. If they don't have a good understanding of how you view your job and priorities, they may have expectations that are very out of line and it can cause bad surprises.

12

Be Data-Driven by the Consumers of Your Product

Kevin Epstein, Author, *Marketing Made Easy*

Always remember, you're not the customer. Even if you are.

As product managers, we all have our favorite features in any product release.

You know what I'm talking about—the UI Panel that's that cool shade of metallic purple, or the way a switch clicks, or the smart tips that appear when the user takes certain actions.

We know in our heart of hearts that **our** feature is what'll really make the product sell. Because, after all, we're consumers of the product, and we know that **we** love this feature. So everyone else will too.

Hence, we fight for the feature.

But we're wrong to do that.

Even if we happen to be right once or twice, statistically we're going to be wrong more often than not. And worse, we probably won't know we're wrong until something about our product is a public failure. (Or, even worse, we don't ever know, the product just won't do well, and we will keep making the same mistake at that or other companies.)

It's like gambling—the house wins in the end. With rare exceptions (Steve Jobs & Co. come to mind), a single person cannot best represent the customer's future needs. The blunt truth is that most product managers are neither perfect samples of the customer base they're representing, nor trend-setting visionaries who can single-handedly design something so brilliant that on seeing it, customers know it's what they have always wanted to own.

Since the goal of product management is to set forth requirements for a successful product—a product that is beloved by users and makes the company ragingly successful—we need to improve our odds of being right about what customers want. We need to be more than one data point. We need to go out and get to know our customers, in both an anecdotal way and a data driven way.

I'd therefore suggest the following simple steps that you can practice on your friends and in the privacy of your own home:

- Go have a meal with your most important customers, and with at least a few customers no one has ever heard of. Why? Food makes people happy and loquacious. Come prepared with a set of five crucial questions, but make sure the first question is always simply, "How's it going, and what sucks?"

- As soon as you're done listening, go find somewhere quiet and write down as much of what they said as you can remember. Taking notes during the chat can disrupt the flow of conversation, so if you are planning to take notes do so respectfully and sparingly, if at all.

- Don't be swayed excessively by passion, noise, or drama on the part of the customer; the loudest yelling or biggest spending customers are often **not** the most representative of the wider base. Also be sure you chat with at least a few customers who've abandoned your product or chosen competitors over you.

- After you've chatted with a lot of folks, and possibly even issued a more formal survey, honestly and rigorously look at the data. Are there trends? What's the pattern behind the comments? What's the root problem to which customers are seeking solution? Remember, it's not about your opinions or their opinions—it's about deep underlying needs. As Ben Horowitz said when I was at Netscape, "Good product managers listen to customers [and] they probe deeper into the underlying problems."

In short—**you** are not the customer, but you **are** the distilled collective voice of **all** of the customers. To paraphrase Stan Lee of Marvel fame (that's comics, not semiconductors): you have a lot of power and a lot of responsibility—act accordingly.

Now, go champion something great.

13

90-360-3

Dan Torres, Senior Director of Global Product
Management, Kensington Computer Products

**The 90-360-3
framework is
designed to gain
critical insights,
visibility, and
measurable
objectives.**

Early in my career as a product manager, I was
asked in an interview, "How long will it take you to
make an impact?" I was caught "off script" and don't
feel I adequately answered the question. It definite-
ly resonated with me to reflect on and to develop a
response. What has come out of that question is a
rule that I sum up as: 90-360-3.

The 90-360-3 framework is designed to gain critical
insights, visibility, and measurable objectives. This
rule can be used whether it is your first day or your
tenth year on the job. The rule breaks down simply:
over ninety days, take a 360-degree view of your
company, and develop three top-line measurable
objectives.

A "first one-hundred days" is pretty much accepted
as a good checkpoint for measuring one's effective-
ness and overall trajectory. Typical business cycles
and critical milestones run quarter to quarter; so, I
find the ninety-day rule a good fit. Ninety days is a
good rule of thumb, but the timing can be modified
to fit other cycles more in tune with your company's
specific rhythms, e.g., weekly, monthly, or even
semi-annually. I don't recommend using this
process beyond six months, since the intent is to
develop a behavior that is agile, perceptive, and effective. Also, too short of a period can result in
knee-jerk responses and unnecessary churn. Find
a rhythm that is effective and sustainable, and
make this a habit.

Central to the role of product manager is assuming
the mantle as "general manager" for all aspects of
your product. Great product managers are always
known to be the one person for any question about
the product. Your product is not just about the final
instance you deliver to a customer. It embodies all

of the decisions, actions, support, etc., that bring it to fruition. The process does not follow a narrow path that begins at the whiteboard and ends at the warehouse. Your role is to ensure a "holistic" product that is beyond the final article a customer holds. It embodies all the efforts of the project such as: research, feature trade-offs, BOM targets, margin contribution, distribution, support, positioning, packaging, etc. In the end, your efforts will translate to customers buying your product, becoming a repeat customer, and being an advocate for your product.

A holistic product can only be accomplished by building up a ritual to reach out to every group within your company. Navigating the various stages of building a product (e.g., ideation, concept testing, business analysis, requirements, development, etc.) there arise discrete times where the input of certain groups over others becomes more critical. However, it is always important to develop 360 degrees of presence, or to perform a walkabout across all groups in your company, even when you are not soliciting specific groups advice or input. Why? At a minimum, it is to

- provide visibility into your product,
- gain any additional or incidental insights from other points of view, and
- connect other company members to add as champions for your product.

Finally, develop a manageable list of at least three key objectives to drive your activities for the next ninety days. These activities should be: attainable, measurable, and impactful.

When it comes to lists, we can all easily become consumed with creating overwhelming lists. Keep things sane. Break things down to approachable tasks that will increase your overall success. Also, compact and focused lists are easier to articulate to management and key stakeholders.

In the end, to make it more flexible for your needs, the 90-360-3 rule can be rephrased as:

- Design a rhythmic timescale right for you and your company.
- Build regular and ongoing connections with all the groups in your company.
- Develop a measurable and attainable set of objectives.

With this simple rule you will be able to create great holistic products for your company and customers.

14 Creativity Opens Up More Possibilities

Natalie Yan-Chatonsky, Product Management Consultant, brainmates pty ltd

Mind mapping aids the process of fundamentally shifting the way you view the issue at hand.

Although apparently at odds with the relatively linear process that product managers follow to manage their products at different stages of the product cycle, creativity is an important aspect of the job. Simple creativity techniques can be used to deal with problems on a day-to-day operational level. They can be applied when trying to solve more complex business issues such as understanding the needs of your target market and how you can address their unmet needs, and ultimately increase market share for your product.

As product managers, we all have tough expectations to meet to make the products we manage be the most competitive in the market and to deliver the highest possible usage rates and revenue growth; and we have to do all this with limited resources and tight timelines. Allowing yourself to tap into your creative instincts can give you the edge to help you successfully deliver on your goals.

One of my favorite tools for problem solving as both a designer and product manager is mind mapping. Start off with a blank sheet of paper and summarize part of the problem you are trying to solve in just one word. This is your starting point for developing multiple associations with the keyword. This simple act of distilling the problem into just one word not only enables you to focus on just one aspect at a time, but also forces you to break down the key drivers of the problem.

With each keyword or concept that you start mind mapping, develop as many branches and sub-branches of keywords associated with the original keyword as possible. This stage of the mind mapping aids the process of fundamentally shifting the way you view the issue at hand. You'll be surprised with the number of concepts you can come up with in a very short amount of time if you let your mind explore all the possibilities that may be totally unrelated to the broader issue that you are trying to solve. Associations on the various branches can be metaphorical. The metaphorical associations are often the source of inspiration for fresh approaches.

When trying to approach more complex problems, mind map as many aspects of the problem as required and select the keywords on the sub-branches that are conceptually strong enough for you to investigate further. The further the sub-branch concepts are from the original keyword, the better.

An alternative to developing new concepts and solutions may be studying parallel universes that are completely unrelated to the product you manage, or even your industry sector. It may be an area of expertise you have in other aspects of your life or an established body of knowledge that you can tap into further through research.

I recently referred to parallel universes when I was developing new market opportunities. I tapped into my role as a mother, considering the unmet needs of parents when it comes to child development, as well as my knowledge of the abundance of educational products that are available to Japanese children that are not available in my local market. The result of this exercise is the initiation of a dialogue with a potential new business partner.

The technique described above can be used individually or collaboratively for problem solving. It's a great way to guide teams to explore all possibilities, without people feeling ridiculed by thinking "outside the square." It enables people to build on each other's ideas constructively, coming up with multiple solutions that you may not have been able to come up with so easily on your own.

Like anything, creativity is developed through practice. Continually practicing methods such as mind mapping and researching parallel universes when trying to come up with original ways of approaching a problem will open up many untapped possibilities. It is an efficient way of discovering alternative approaches and fresh marketing messaging, as well as delivering unique solutions during the problem solving process—all critical aspects of the product manager's role.

15

Get Your Hands Dirty

**John Cook, VP of Consumer PC Marketing,
Hewlett Packard Company**

**People who
can practice
theoretical
product
management are
a dime a dozen.
Those who
shine are the ones
who have that
"aha" moment.**

You must be willing to get your hands dirty if you want to be a great product manager. I'm still amazed at the number of product mangers that seem to have little or no interest in actually using the product or service they're developing. Some seem just as happy to go through the motions of the job with little or no passion and zero personal insights into what they're marketing. For some project managers, it's just a job it seems. And they could care less whether they're making a new salad dressing or developing the next killer phone. You see, there's nothing wrong being the product manager for a new salad dressing, but you better be taking home test batches and trying it on yourself before you test it on the public. Do you use your products every day? Do you contribute to bug count? Have you ever broken a hardware proto-type? If you're not, you're not doing your job.

Just how do you expect to be credible with engi-neering, your manager, or even your peers if you're not passionate about what you're building? Being passionate means actually having an opinion and insights that can only be gained from actually hacking, cracking, and beating on the very thing you're trying to develop.

With few exceptions (I have friends that develop surgical robots, for example), you must find a way to install the pre-alpha software, to test the earliest version of your new cloud service, or to break the latest prototype that engineering has. This is not optional. It's a big (and important) part of your job to get inside your customer's head. Don't just talk about the "voice of the customer." Be the customer.

Yes, yes, it's a "survey of one," but it's absolutely necessary to being conversant and being able to more passionately (there's that word again) support your business proposition.

I've found that people who can practice theoretical product management are a dime a dozen. Those who shine are the ones who have that "aha" moment getting too caught up in their own work, the product managers who clearly understand the limitations of their product and who discover the hidden elegance that only comes of time and repetition.

When I first came to Silicon Valley, I worked for Apple. Even back in the day, the competition for jobs there was fierce. I had flown out from the East Coast where I worked for a large mainframe company. In my briefcase was a nicely printed copy of my resume and a floppy disk. I had written a program using Apple's recently announced programming tool, HyperCard, to show off my skills with the Mac as well as how we should "eat our own dog food" when it came to gathering customer requirements.

In every interview there, I brought out the disk and offered to showcase my talents. Would you believe that not a single person in the department had HyperCard installed on their Mac or enough RAM to run the program? I got the job (partially because of that disk I believe), but the sad fact I discovered was that the disk could have been blank. No one was actually using the technology they had just announced and were continuing to develop and promote. We changed that when I came onboard. Everyone got equipment to take home, have on their desks and even share with friends and family when it made sense.

Two lessons I learned: I always ask about a candidate's best hands-on experiences when I'm interviewing and always make sure my department practices what we preach.

16

Get Out of the Office

Paula Gray, Applied Cultural
Anthropologist, AIPMM

Markets do not buy products, people do; businesses do not buy products, people (several, or a group, but always people) do.

It is our natural tendency to overestimate the importance that our product holds within the lives of our customers. Spend some time to see firsthand where your product fits into the holistic picture of a customer's life.

The Whole Picture

A good product manager can access loads of data. You can review market research demographics, sales numbers, and product specs to name a few, and all of these are valuable. But remember, the product, company, processes, and ultimate purpose of your job all exist to sell customers products they want to buy. That perspective puts customers in charge and there is no better way to learn about customers than by observing their behavior in their own natural environment. Focus groups, interviews, and surveys are valuable, but they only offer part of the picture. You need to go to where the customers are, and that involves getting out of your cubicle or office.

The Customer as a Source of Insight

In generations past, organizations held a "producer's view of the world," where customers and the marketplace were viewed as part of the system outside the business, a destination that products and services were sent outward **to**. Many times, organizations created products first and then looked for customers afterward, dictating what the customer would have to accept. Now, due to increased competition, the customer is gaining their rightful place in the process. The customer is viewed as a valuable source of innovation to draw

from. This more enlightened view of the value of the customer, and the need for exchanges with them, has transformed the way consumer behavior is studied, analyzed and acted upon.[vi]

Outdated is the practice of simply describing the customers' purchase decision such as who buys what, where, and what factors influence the decision. Most product managers and marketers now recognize that statistical analysis of survey data related to consumer demographics makes their customer a number on a spreadsheet, or a point on a graph, and leaves them far short of enough valuable data. Now, firms are interested in "gaining a holistic understanding of consumers' lives in context, and finding out what this may teach them about new opportunities to create or improve products, or how to make new sales."[vii]

It is important to recognize that a market is a grouping of **people** who share some similar human behaviors such as particular buying or usage patterns. Assessing or defining the market requires an understanding of **human** behavior. Markets do not buy products, **people** do; businesses do not buy products, **people** (several, or a group, but always people) do. Go beyond "personas," which are fictional characters, and connect with "persons" who are living, breathing customers.

So how do you do that?

Grab Your Keys and Head for the Door

There is no other way than to simply go spend time with customers. If you sell to consumers, go where people shop or where they "hang out." Watch, listen, and look for patterns. What are their topics of conversation, what are they seeing from their perspective, how are they behaving, how long does it take them to select a product?

If you sell to businesses, volunteer to go on customer visits or sales calls and be an astute listener and observer. What is hanging on the wall of your customer's office? What key words does your customer repeat? How is the office arranged?

These observations can yield insights into the purchase decision process, the "ranking" of important issues, and even what your product symbolizes for your customer. Incredibly valuable information not revealed in the charts, graphs and spreadsheets sitting on your desk back in the office.

You Do Not Own Your Product

Linda Merrick, Founder, Pivotal PM

The difference between leading your product team and owning every aspect of every detail in your product is your level of sanity.

As product managers, we're encouraged to act as CEOs for our products. What does that really mean? Many of us believe that it means we should be making all the decisions about our products. After all, how can you be responsible for its success if you don't have this authority?

But watch your CEO carefully. If the CEO in your company is making all the decisions, then

1. you're not making product decisions anyway, the CEO is; and

2. this is not a very scalable company.

I've seen product managers who want to make all the decisions—and I've been one. We drive ourselves crazy trying to be everywhere at once, wasting emotional energy when decisions are made without us, and creating a huge bottleneck the rest of the time.

Successful leaders at all levels know that collaborative decision making is more effective than top-down mandates. Here are my top rules about facilitating product decisions:

- Define the right criteria for the decision. This is the key to the product manager's role in decision making. Work with your team to make sure you understand what will influence their decision and what data they need to see.

- Get all points of view on the table. Even if the decision made doesn't favor a particular view, at least that input gets acknowledged.

- Think through the implications (strategic, financial, tactical/logistics) from each perspective you've heard.
- In most decisions, some stakeholders will hold a larger or more critical stake than others. Make sure you identify the key stakeholders to the team. Get them to provide data and do your own research to provide any missing data.
- Present data and other facts to the team, in context of the strategy and financials.
- Look to your key stakeholders to propose solutions and ask for the team's support. You can also propose your own solution.
- Map out a Plan B and help your team understand how you will determine if the recommended approach is working (or not), and how you will transition to Plan B if needed.
- Ask for support. You'll likely find that even those who don't agree with the recommended decision will go along with it. They've had a chance to provide input, they understand which functional group has the most at stake, they've seen the supporting data, and they know how the team will take corrective action if needed.

NOTE: There may be times when your team turns to you to and asks you to make the decision. When they ask, do it. But still follow the process above so that you have good information as the basis for your decision, and as much buy-in as possible.

What if a functional group needs to make a decision relating to your product and can't bring it to you or the team? If they know your strategy, they'll be much more likely to make the right decision.

Collaborative decision making is just plain smart. Why forgo the incredible amount of experience and expertise on your cross-functional team? Leverage it and your product will be well on its way to success. And your life will be a lot less crazy.

18

Carve Out "Think" Time

Adrienne Tan, Director, brainmates pty ltd

Product managers—carve out some "think" time in your busy day to be more productive and to deliver better results.

Product managers are often overwhelmed by day-to-day operational and tactical responsibilities. Urgent tasks such as reporting, solving urgent customer queries, responding to the sales groups, and reviewing marketing collateral are constantly on the product manager's agenda. Product managers repeatedly say that they have little time to focus on the important, more strategic activities that generate real value for the business.

Whilst it's almost impossible to stop supporting the product at the operational level, it's vital that product managers carve out "think" time in their working week or month.

So What Does "Think" Time Actually Mean?

"Think" time is essentially about taking a moment to consider the long-term prospects of the product, explore new markets, discover untapped opportunities, learn about alternative product solutions, and up-skill on product management techniques. It's reflective, quiet time to step aside from the day-to-day machinations of supporting the product.

As a product management consultant working on a project for a cable television channel in Australia, I noticed that producers and editors made an effort to carve out some free time from their tight daily television production schedules. They used what they called "think" time to dream of fresh story lines, explore new ways to promote existing television content, and generally took time away from their desks to refresh their minds and to help think creatively.

The Serious Side of "Think" Time

The strategic role of the product manager is complex and requires quiet time to consider and reflect on customer problems, the direction of the market, and the strategic path and alignment of the product against the business strategy. Sitting at a desk responding to operational problems or preparing that all important slide pack for senior management leaves little time for product managers to consider or uncover innovative solutions to these issues.

"Think" time is productive time. The benefits may not be immediate but are enormous. The benefit of "think" time is evident across many industries and professions.

Stefan Sagmeister, a New York designer and TED 2009 speaker, closes his studio and takes a sabbatical every seven years. The time out, he says, not only gives him the opportunity to rejuvenate but enables him to develop innovative design solutions to common problems.

Ferran Adria an infamous Spanish chef opens his restaurant El Bulli seven months of the year. The other five months he spends experimenting with new cooking techniques and ingredients. As a result, El Bulli is one of the most successful restaurants, receiving two million reservation requests per year.

3M ensures that their engineers set aside 15 percent of their time to engage in any desired activity in the workplace. Scotch Tape® and Post-it Notes® were created as a result of this downtime.

With a little "think" time, the product manager is ultimately a better product manager for the company, the benefits of which manifest in profitable products that deliver greater business value and a competitive advantage in the marketplace.

Pencil In "Think" Time Now

Product managers must make a conscious effort to set aside some time in their work schedule to allow for "think" time. As a start, pencil in a two-hour meeting every month for "think" time and, as this activity becomes familiar, increase the frequency of "think" time to every week.

Spend "think" time reading an inspiring book, catching up on your favorite blogs, sketching new product ideas, tinkering with new software, and talking to leaders outside of the product management profession or to a leader working in a different industry. An essential aspect of "think" time is to step away from direct product management tasks.

More importantly, the product manager must commit to continue "think" time in busy periods. This commitment eventually derives results that are similar to those of 3M's and others.

Product managers remember that always "doing" may not necessarily generate profitable results or lead down the desired path.

19

Get the Market Segmentation Right!

David Fradin, Senior
Principal Consultant, 280 Group

Getting the market segmentation right is oftentimes the key contributor to success or failure. This is particularly difficult when trying to address an emerging market.

Apple

At Apple in 1983, after demonstrating sufficient product management and marketing skills in bringing the first hard disk drive to market for a personal computer, the Personal Computer Systems Division asked me to take over as the Apple III Group Product Manager. I replaced some pretty good product managers: Trip Hawkins who started Electronic Arts, Rob Campbell who founded the company that invented PowerPoint and File-Maker, and the original product manager for the Apple III-Steve Jobs.

At the time, corporate marketing had segmented the market into home and business with nothing in between. The concept of small office/home office (SOHO) had not yet emerged.

I studied how the Apple III was being used. It had a larger spreadsheet (Super VisiCalc) than any other PC, solid word processing from Quark, a real keyboard to fall in love with, and other advanced features. The product was perfect for the yet to be defined SOHO market. PC market penetration was just 4 percent.

We spent our entire marketing budget going after our definition for SOHO, resulting in the sales of twenty-three thousand Apple IIIs for a gross revenue of $60 million, thus making the installed base of about seventy-five thousand the third largest of any mini/microcomputers just after the Apple II and the DEC PDP 11.

Lesson: *Do your own market segmentation and then focus your product marketing on that segmentation.*

Digital F/X

In 1990, Digital F/X invented the first desktop video editing system that enabled a Macintosh computer to control tape decks for editing along with a video switcher and character generator. They thought the market for it was people who knew how to use a computer but had never made videos before. They expected to sell thousands per month just like the Truevision video card (a leading third-party video card at the time).

When I took over as the second product manager, I talked to customers and found that our product was being purchased by video professionals because it cut the cost of a video editing suite from $150,000 to about $70,000. As a result, the total available market was only about twelve thousand. But due to poor market segmentation, the company had already spent about $20 million in manufacturing thousands of units, assuming that the market was much larger. They also spent $250,000 on a user's guide, explaining in vivid detail all the things video professionals already knew how to do—except how to use a computer.

Result: *This VC backed company went out of business, in part because management refused to understand their customer and segment the market correctly.*

Large File Transfer SaaS (Software-as-a-Service) Company

The company introduced a product with the name "corporate" in it and then wondered why the product was not selling as well as it was forecasted to sell. Multiple sales people and sales management came in and were fired because they weren't making their sales quota selling to "enterprises."

Later, they learned two-fifths of their market was government and education who, upon looking at a product's name, said, "We are not corporate, so a corporate product won't work for us." In addition, the product that was built lacked the features/functions required by corporate enterprise customers.

Lesson: *Align the product with the market segments using common sense, not what you wish. Monitor sales wins and losses. Talk to real customers to check the assumptions. Be willing to change.*

So How Do You Accurately Segment Your Market?

Look at the market. Talk to the prospective customers. Find groupings that match common **needs, characteristics, and behavior.**

List them out. Work and rework. Brainstorm with others. Conduct face-to-face interviews, surveys, polls, and focus groups. Look at how your competitors segment the market. If your market is in the United States, consider using the NAICS database for industry and labor classifications to get your arms around the total market. Step back from your draft segmentation. Ask if this makes sense. Is it clear? Easily understood? Does it map into the real world?

20 Clarify Product Positioning

Fritz Mueller, Senior Director of Product Management, i365

The positioning statement provides the first decision filter because it defines what you are, and any idea either needs to reinforce that identity or move you down a path defined by your vision.

An essential starting point for solving many product management problems is a clear positioning statement. In every company there is a constant dialogue of ideas from sales, marketing, and development on how to improve sales, handle changes in the market, and beat competitors. Combine this situation with limited resources and you are forced to figure out the best set of trade-offs. Most of the ideas will have some merit in isolation, so you need a good filter through which to keep, modify, and discard ideas. The positioning statement provides the first filter because it defines what you are and any idea either needs to reinforce that identity or move you down a path defined by your vision. Everything else is a distraction, or the basis for a new product.

The positioning statement is what you say if someone with a minimal understanding of your industry asks what your product is. If you had to answer in one sentence, then whatever you say is your positioning (or is derived from it). If I had to guess the positioning statement for McDonald's, it would be the "world's largest fast food chain." From those five words my listener knows that it is a restaurant chain, but not high-end, the company is all about market reach, it is not a specialty chain, it competes internationally, and it is number one in market share. At this point, the listener has the big picture and everything else I say fills in details.

Creating a positioning statement forces you to figure out what you are best at, where you are in the hierarchy, and exactly what you are selling. If you don't like your answer for any of those three elements then you have a good idea where you need improvement. A good statement also helps you filter all the ideas that need to be taken seriously and which should be rejected. This includes pricing, promotions, target market, partnerships, feature sets, etc. Once you know where your weakness is, then you know where to focus attention.

It is likely you are already using this process intuitively, but doing it more explicitly will help you defend your decisions, especially if you are rejecting an idea that sounds good in general but does not feel right for your particular product. Chasing mediocre ideas is always a drain on resources, but it is hard to reject them unless you have a better idea or can show that they will not solve the real problem.

To write a good statement, start with the following questions:

• Where do you provide value?
• What are you the best at in the industry?
• What exactly do you sell?

Now write the long version of the positioning statement, a couple paragraphs if necessary. This gets the idea into writing and captures the important elements. Next, start refining it to a few sentences and finally one sentence. The longer versions will be useful, so keep them. The exercise will generally force you to think about your vision, your limitations, the market, and your competitors. If sales are lackluster, there is a good chance you are in a weak market or your rank in a good market is too low to thrive. Your goal is to position yourself as number one in some market segment, a position of strength from which you can grow.

21
Define and Align Your Roles and Responsibilities

Tom Evans,
Principal Consultant, Lûcrum Marketing

As there are many perspectives on the product management role, make sure your definition is aligned with that of your new management team.

One of the great challenges of taking on a new product management role at a company is the many definitions and perspectives of what product management is and what the roles are called. And it doesn't help that the job description used for the role was probably cut and pasted from somewhere without much thought as to what was really required. Based upon my experience of taking on new product management roles, one important lesson that I learned is to make sure that your understanding of the role and your management's understanding of the role are well aligned. Any significant misalignment will result in significant frustration and dissatisfaction.

To illustrate with one example, I joined a small technology company as the first product manager ever. I saw this as a great opportunity to establish and grow the role within the organization. During an early meeting with the CEO, I talked about scheduling some customer visits and his response was, "if you want to learn what our customers need, just ask me." In his mind, my only job was to write product requirements and there was no need for me to speak with customers, because he already knew it. As I continued to define and grow the product management role, I butted heads far too often with the CEO, and this opportunity turned into a very painful experience. Now this is probably an extreme case of role misalignment, but any major misalignment between you and your management team will most likely turn into a negative experience.

So what can you do to avoid this situation? As you start interviewing for a new role, enter with a strong definition of what you expect the role to be and discuss this with the interviewing team. If you're not sure how to do this, start with the foundation you learned in your product management training. Pull out that framework that you have tucked away, build your definition of the role based upon that framework, and then augment that with your past experience of what worked and didn't work. From this exercise, you should have a pretty good definition of the product management role. Discuss this with everyone you interview with, especially the hiring manager, product management peers and cross-functional peers (engineering, marketing, sales, etc.). This will accomplish two things for you. It will ensure that your vision of the role matches the vision of your management and colleagues. If it doesn't align, this opens up a good opportunity for a healthy discussion that will help you find a middle ground that meets everyone's expectations. This discussion will also underscore your depth of knowledge and experience in the product management role and help set you apart.

If you only discover this misalignment once you get into the new role, the first step I recommend is to do what I described above. Build your definition of the product management role based upon your training and experience and then start discussing it with the management team. You should discover either that they don't have a full understanding of the role or that you have differing definitions of the role. From my experience, most often the case is that they don't have a full understanding of the product management role, and this is your opportunity to educate them on what you should be doing and why you should be doing it. Build a plan on how you'll implement your vision of the role and then execute on it, keeping clear and open communications with management during the full process.

If all of this fails, I highly recommend you start looking for another opportunity, as the current situation can only set you back in your career progression.

22

Write It Down!

Sarah Rosenbaum Gaeta; Senior Director of
Content Product Management & Sales
Enablement, Plastic Logic

To be the product leader—which a good product manager is—you need a record.

Nothing is worse than a product manager who keeps everything in their head and shares nothing materially with others. Your job is to document, document, document, and then go back and clarify, clarify, clarify. Your PRDs (product requirements documents) and MRDs (market requirements documents) should be **the** go-to information sources for **everyone** working on the product or supporting the product in some way. You need to educate, persuade, coach, and manage internal and external perceptions, assumptions, and people. To do this, have every pertinent piece of information documented. You can measure your success by the frequency people quote or refer to your documents. Give it to them—they need it.

To be the product leader—which a good product manager is—you need a record. Without it, others will try to mold the product into their view, which may not align well with what the market needs and the opportunity you're chasing. Here are a few steps to creating a written record for your product:

1. Determine who your audiences are and what they need to learn from the document(s).

2. Determine in what time frame these audiences need to be served. For example, maybe engineering is the most urgent audience. If so, then it may be best to begin with the PRD sections for engineering and then move onto other areas of the PRD or the MRD.

3. Invite reviews and inputs. You are most successful when others feel ownership and accomplishment for your document. You want and need to be recognized as being the primary contributor, not the scribe. However, allow-

ing others to contribute creates a community of ownership and belief; and that can serve the process very well later when tough decisions and prioritizations need to be made.

4. Post it where anyone in the company can get to it easily (assuming there's no information that requires a restricted distribution list). Many CEOs and VPs I know troll the intranet/corporate network looking for "interesting" items to read. Wouldn't it be great if your CEO commented to your VP that she'd read the PRD or MRD? The fact that a CEO takes the time to do that reflects well on you. It also provides visibility for upper management, which is good. A lack of visibility usually raises doubt and uncertainty in people's minds.

5. Revise and update as needed, and in a timely fashion. If a major area of the product was put on hold, then update the document ASAP. Don't let it get too out of date or the credibility of the record goes down with the accuracy. This can be a slippery, fast slope down, and then you find you're not the product manager anymore.

This doesn't mean you have to be the lone author. Create a documentation team and coordinate the activities. When a good team is brought together to author a PRD or MRD, the outcome can be astoundingly thorough, clear, and complete. Set your sights high and tap the best and most appropriate talent to participate.

23 Make Sure You Have Clear Priorities

Dan Olsen, Co-Founder and CEO, YourVersion

The best product teams are crystal clear about their priorities at every point in time and are adept at quickly changing their priorities when they need to.

Make Sure You Have Clear Priorities

We've all seen PRDs that list ten (or more) "high priority" product features. What are feature lists like this really saying? They're really saying, "We weren't sure about our priorities," or, "Nobody made the tough calls about which features were really most important."

Why Are Clear Priorities Important?

There are always more product ideas than there are resources to implement them. To maximize a company's business results and chances of success, it needs to have a clear point of view about what's most important. When there are ten "high priority" features, how does engineering know which one to start working on first? How does the rest of the team know which one engineering is going to work on first?

Different stakeholders can look at a list of ten high priority features and mistakenly expect that their top item will get launched soon, especially when engineering only has the resources to work on one or two items at a time. In contrast, having clear priorities ensures that everyone in the company is clear on what is going to get done in what order.

The lack of clear priorities is often a symptom of one or more problems:

- The team doesn't have a clear point of view about what is most important to its success or to its customers.
- People on the team have clear opinions about what's most important but can't agree.

- Nobody is empowered to make tough product decisions.
- The team lacks the right processes or tools.

The first three problems are all rooted in the company culture, and that can be hard to change, so I'll share advice on how product managers can improve on the final problem.

Make a List

The first step is to create a prioritized feature list. Each feature should be listed as a separate item on its own row. You should assign a priority level to each feature such as "high," "medium," and "low." However, it's also important to individually rank-order the features **within each priority level**. Within the "high" features, decide which one is #1, which is #2, and so on. You can use shorthand labels like "H-1," "H-2," "M-1," "M-2," "L-1," "L-2." Your list should always be sorted by that rank-order priority. If you're not empowered to determine the rank-order priority yourself, then facilitate the process to do so with the key stakeholders. Once you have a prioritized list, it makes your life a lot easier when the time comes to make tough trade-offs. For example, the next time someone comes to you with a new "top priority" idea, just whip out the list and ask them to tell you which "lower priority" items can afford to get bumped.

Share the List and Keep It Updated

The prioritized feature list should be easily accessible by everyone so that the entire team is on the same page. Just because the list has precise priorities doesn't mean it has to be rigid; it should be updated real-time as new features come up and priorities change. A "live" web-based list works much better than sending revised lists by email over and over. Don't let your tracking tools get in the way, just keep it simple: Google spreadsheets or wikis work great.

"Be Water, My Friend"

A team with rank-ordered priorities in place can react more quickly when changes arise. The best product teams are crystal clear about their priorities at every point in time and are adept at quickly changing their priorities when they need to. So when it comes to product priorities, as Bruce Lee said, "Be water, my friend": clear and agile.

24
Salespeople Don't Just Want to Make Lots of Money

Dave Dersh, VP of Consulting
and Training, 280 Group

Helping salespeople win is a primary role of the product marketing team!

Marketing often refers to salespeople as being "coin operated." While it's true that a large portion of a salesperson's income is tied directly to what they sell, money is **not** the only thing that motivates them. First and foremost, salespeople want to **win**! Salespeople are competitive by nature, and winning gratifies their egos and enriches their bank accounts. Money is just one way of keeping score.

Helping salespeople win is a primary role of the product marketing team. Helping the sales team is not just about fancy data sheets or slick presentations, but it must include a deep understanding of the customer buying process. For example, why do customers buy our products or services vs. competitors? Who are the *real* buyers vs. end users? What are the customer problems, issues, and needs that our product or service solves? What is unique about our product or service that the competition truly cannot match, and how does this tie back to the customer's value equation?

If the truth be told, salespeople use very little of what product marketing provides. This is mainly because it focuses on generic features and benefits and not what the **salesperson's** customer views as unique value.

Want to really help your salespeople win? Here are a few suggestions:

- Go on sales calls and ask prospects and customers what **their** definition of "value" is (not yours).
- Spend time getting to know various sales representatives, their customers, selling styles, etc.

- Read the win/loss analyses included in most customer relationship management (CRM) systems. Knowing why a deal was lost can often be more valuable than knowing why it was won.
- Ask salespeople if they actually use any of the sales collateral. You might be surprised!
- Get sales feedback on products and promotions **before** you launch.
- Always reach out to salespeople **before** you speak with their customers. Nothing irks salespeople more than knowing you've spoken to their customer(s) after the fact.
- If you are a product manager pitching to a prospect or existing customer, meet with the salesperson **before** the sales presentation. The salesperson can help you zero in on customer value definition, competitive situation, etc.

As an example, I was once involved in a situation where a product manager pitched a new high-tech product to a prospect. It was a new product category, and we were both anxious to tell the prospect why our offering was superior. The product manager was briefed about the customer situation beforehand. However, it became obvious that the product manager was more interested in discussing the product's unique features, most of which provided very little unique business value to **that** prospect. The presentation did not go well and the sale was lost to the competition. Suffice it to say that I never put that product manager in front of a prospect again.

In summary, salespeople are motivated primarily by winning. Money is simply a yardstick to keep score. Focusing on your product or service features and benefits without tying these directly to **business value** is a recipe for failure. In the example above, the product manager might have spent more time really getting to know the prospect (perhaps by taking me to lunch) or going on a sales call early in the buying process. Had he done so, it might have helped him better tie back to the customer's value equation or present a better approach if his offering could not solve the customer's problem (i.e., changing the rules). In any case, understanding what really motivates most salespeople will help win acceptance and drive more revenue for your products and services.

25 Create a Culture of Openness

Eric Krock, Chief Marketing Officer, Voximate

It's not the land mine you know about that will kill you; it's the one that you don't know about.

As a product manager, you will not see all of the greatest dangers or opportunities yourself, so you must create a culture of openness within your company. Only open communication will ensure that dangers are avoided and opportunities are capitalized on.

At one employer, I was asked to take over the product management team after a restructuring. So I asked every member of the remaining team (myself included) to divide up a list of people in all functional units and ask them in private one-on-one meetings how they felt about the team's recent performance.

We found many opportunities for improvement. Engineering said the current server schedule was unachievable. A team review showed they were right; we had to slip the delivery date by four months. Sales said their input hadn't always been solicited in the product planning process, and engineering said that product management decisions had sometimes been made arbitrarily. No security review had been done on the plan for rewriting the client, so I convened one. In the first five minutes, the sales engineers reported that a simplifying assumption in the client plan would be unacceptable to our enterprise customers, so I had to throw out that plan and slip the client delivery date by six months.

I also went to our major customers and privately asked for their input. Some said that in recent months they'd stopped hearing from the company and felt ignored.

To fix the product planning and delivery process, we created a culture of radical openness. I asked the IT group to deploy a wiki and began tracking every open issue within it for all in the company to see. I required that every product release plan be reviewed and approved by engineering, quality assurance, sales, and the executive team internally, and by all our major customers externally. We didn't **assume** our plans would please customers; we confirmed it. We didn't **assume** that engineering, QA, and sales had had the opportunity to voice any concerns; we ensured it. I personally reviewed the mock-ups for the major client rewrite screen-by-screen with our major enterprise customers to ensure they'd be willing to deploy it to their tens of thousands of desktops when it was released.

We didn't just solicit input; we acted on it. We ensured that release schedules included realistic adequate buffer room to ensure there was time to deal with the inevitable surprises along the way.

The results were extraordinary. The company went from not knowing it was six months behind schedule to shipping the next thirteen releases in a row on or ahead of schedule. Every customer accepted the delivery of every release and feature we delivered to them, and we won every deal that was contingent upon the delivery of new functionality. We closed a record number of new customers, became profitable for the first time, and more than tripled the company's valuation in just eighteen months.

But I'm happiest of all about the results of the annual employee survey we conducted at the end of this period. Ninety-five percent agreed that "everyone has the opportunity to express their opinions," "after the debate, we move forward and support decisions made," and "we foster open and direct communication." Ninety percent agreed that "we focus on listening and understanding," "we challenge each other's thinking to get the best idea/solution," and "we communicate early and often." These numbers had doubled since the previous year. Not only were we performing better, but everyone felt included in a rational, open process. This was no coincidence.

26 Align Your Product Strategy with the Company Strategy—Then Sell It

Mara Krieps, Founder, Pivotal PM

Your product needs executive sponsorship to succeed. You gain executive sponsorship by showing how your product strategy supports the company strategy.

The intrepid product manager who masters this rule will follow three steps: 1) understanding the company strategy, 2) aligning product strategy with company strategy, and 3) telling the strategy story and gaining executive support.

First, you need to understand the company strategy.

Sometimes your company's strategy is easy to find. Some organizations do an excellent job of communicating the mission and strategy to all employees on a regular basis. Ben and Jerry's comes to mind as a great example of clear communication of company mission and strategy.[viii]

But in most companies the strategy is a partial or complete mystery. I've worked in many fast-moving organizations where it changed frequently, and/or the executive team didn't communicate it well. (Names withheld to protect the culpable.) In those cases, I've had to engage in some creative sleuthing.

Here are a few tips for gaining clarity on your company's current strategy:

Find the "breadcrumb trails." Hunt down presentations from recent divisional or company meetings, or find recent emails from executive team members; these often include at least a hint about the current company strategy.

I also like taking advantage of informal moments, like hallway conversations, to ask an executive, "What are you working on?" Their answer to the question can yield revealing clues to what's strategically important now.

Share some data, gain some insight. Whenever you have new information on the market, the competition, and your customers, you have the basis for a strategy conversation with an information-hungry executive team member. Executives like quoting market data that supports their plans—even if it's anecdotal. So find an opportunity to contribute some of your market knowledge, then look for a natural segue in the conversation to ask strategy related questions.

When all else fails, follow the money. Identifying where your company is making money or spending money is the clearest way to locate the **real** strategy, even if the **stated** strategy is something completely different. If you have access to your company's financials, spend some time combing through the detail, or schedule time with the controller, CFO, or an analyst in finance to get some clarity and guidance.

Note that "following the money" includes finding the basis for executive team bonuses, which tells you what your senior managers are most likely to care about this year. For example, if an executive has signed up for an aggressive customer acquisition target per the bonus plan, you can bet that her focus will be on winning new customers!

Second, align your product strategy with company strategy.

Your product strategy must support the company's ability to deliver on its current strategy; if not, your product will be seen as diverting resources away from the "greater good." Based on my own experience, this kind of nonalignment can provide exciting opportunities to advocate for changing the whole company's direction but, in most cases, it's not a fun—or career enhancing—position to be in. For a great example of nonalignment, do a quick Web search on the Cadillac Catera (remember "the Caddie that Zigs?") and shudder.

So, once you are clear about the company strategy, work with your cross-functional team to develop a product strategy that makes sense in the context of the company's current goals.

What's the best way to clarify and begin documenting a product strategy? Wrap your mind around the market, product, communication, pricing, and channel, then take a quick "essay test."

Third, tell your strategy story and gain executive support.

With your product strategy in place, it's time to schedule a few "testing the waters" conversations with key executives. Take their feedback and make any needed adjustments, then unveil the product strategy to the full executive team and ask for the resources you need to make the product strategy real.

Follow these steps and watch all of your homework pay off!

27 Short, Standardized Cycle Times Drive Predictability

James Moorehead, VP of Product Management, Support.com

I've found predictability to be more important than high productivity.

Every product manager wants to be the bearer of good news, sharing details of on-time product releases packed with high value features. Too often, however, product managers bear news of yet another late release or the feature that had to be scoped out. When customers, partners, and internal constituents lose confidence in a development organization's ability to consistently deliver promised functionality, the inevitable outcome is micromanagement and second-guessing of the product organization. With over a decade of product management experience, using both waterfall and agile methodologies, I've found predictability to be more important than high productivity. Knowing that what gets prioritized and accepted into a development cycle gets released into production on time, every time.

Predictability means dependent organizations —internal and external—can plan with confidence (and without feeling the need to backseat drive the product organization). Business executives will choose slightly less functionality in exchange for higher predictability almost every time. Like many product development organizations, my current organization struggled in the past with releasing the committed scope of functionality on schedule. Over the past few years, however, we've released on time and in-scope 90+ percent of the time.

How did we calculate the 90 percent success metric? We looked back at actual release dates vs. planned release dates, and also looked at cases where a feature accepted into a sprint (using Scrum as our development approach) wasn't production ready. Exceptions existed in less than 10 percent of cases—a dramatic improvement from our level of predictability when we were following three to six month waterfall development cycles.

The switch to agile development (Scrum specifically) was a major factor in achieving this high level of predictability. Under the hood of Scrum, however, it has been our refinement of development cycle times that has had the most impact. We started with very tight cycles—two weeks—but found we were consistently late. We bumped up to three weeks per sprint but still found it difficult to achieve predictability. Development cycles that are too short don't leave sufficient time for QA and refinement. We ultimately settled on a standardized four-week cycle, with one week in between sprints for planning, enabling nine to ten major releases per calendar year. (Note that four-week cycles are working weeks, not calendar weeks, allowing holidays to be taken into account on a sprint-by-sprint basis.)

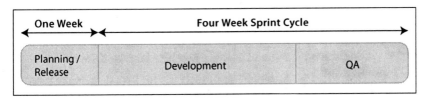

Why did a standardized, four-week sprint cycle have such an impact? Both "standardized" and "four week" are important. By standardizing on a cycle, our product management, engineering, and QA teams have found a rhythm—a natural feel for what can be accomplished in a four-week cycle. Four weeks has proven effective because it is long enough for significant progress on features, but short enough to be estimated accurately. Four weeks is also short enough from a business perspective that the risk of mid-sprint executive overrides (changes in priorities) is minimized. We've been able to avoid this problem altogether. The most significant challenge with three to six month waterfall cycles is estimating the work—like many companies, we simply couldn't achieve sufficient accuracy in estimation over such a long cycle, resulting in low predictability.

I noted above that predictability is more important than high productivity. The hidden gem here is that predictability, in our experience, drives higher productivity because as the product teams deliver consistently, confidence in the ability to delivery grows—and the teams are prepared to take on more each sprint cycle. By focusing first on predictability we have ultimately achieved higher productivity.

What product manager would argue with that outcome?

28

Find Market Problems Worth Solving

Nick Coster, Director, brainmates pty ltd

Visioning allows the product manager to see beyond what is currently considered possible and to start to think of completely new possibilities.

A lot of people come up with new ideas all the time. Unfortunately, most of these ideas never make it to market because the underlying problem has not been clearly thought out and communicated. It may seem obvious that we would want to understand a potential problem before launching a product to solve it. Sadly, the reality is quite different.

A better approach is to invest time to clearly describe the problem you have identified and then imagine a world where it has been solved. Observe your target market trying to complete tasks and ask yourself ridiculous questions that smash the limits of their current expectations.

Find market problems that are worth solving.

This is often the hardest part of our job. We can get so close to our products that we no longer have the wide view to see market problems that are bigger than problems that are currently being addressed. Instead, we see the world through our products and often add new features to further enhance solutions to problems that have already been adequately solved. For a product manager, it is not the value of the technology that will add value to the business, it is the value of solving the market problem.

How do we find market problems worth solving? Watch people. See what they do and what frustrates them, wastes their time or money, or otherwise prevents them from completing a task that they are trying to perform. Listen to see if this is a pain point for other people.

James Dyson, for example, observed that vacuums were constantly getting clogged with dust and were losing suction. This was a problem for anyone wanting to quickly and effectively clean their house. After over five thousand failed attempts, he created the Dyson vacuum cleaner—a bagless vacuum that doesn't lose suction as it picks up dust.

Describe the pain point that you find, tell a story about it, and describe the specific target market "persona," then step them through the way that they currently try to complete their task. It should be as specific as possible and highlight the impact of their current "solution" in these current usage scenarios.

Imagine a world where the problem has already been solved.

This is the core of most good science fiction. Take a problem that has been solved by some advanced technology and explore the resulting world or environment.

Apply the usage scenario where the pain point was identified and imagine the experience where it has been removed. What is that worth to the target market? Does it create a valuable change in these people's lives? If it does, then there may be merit in actually finding a solution to the problem.

Don't be discouraged if the solution seems impossible.

Most of the products that we use trivially today have been considered impossible at some stage in the past. You may need to sell the vision to stakeholders to get their commitment. If the vision is clear enough, you will find people who want to work with you rather than tell you what can't be done.

The benefit however of knowing that you have a valuable problem that is worth solving is that any effort that you do direct towards creating something new will have a clear market when it is solved and will minimize wasted effort.

Solving problems like this will create new value for the customer, make it difficult for the competition to catch up and create financial opportunities for the business.

A Business Is Not a Democracy

Phil Burton, Senior
Principal Consultant, 280 Group

If you don't make the difficult decisions, chances are no one will, and the business will suffer as a result.

As a product manager, you have a unique role within the company. No one else within the company has the overall view of the entire business through the lens of your product that you do—not the CEO, not the finance people, not the manufacturing people, not the sales people, and not engineering. People in these job roles view your product through the perspective of their own job responsibilities and professional focuses.

As a product manager, your overall view can be a great source of job satisfaction. But you also have a unique responsibility for making decisions and recommendations about your product. As a product manager, you generally have no real authority (unless you manage a product management team), so all you can really do is make recommendations and influence people by the strength of your ideas and work. If you don't make the difficult decisions, chances are no one will, and the business will suffer as a result.

People in various job roles will always make decisions that make their jobs as easy as possible or more interesting. It's human nature. For example, how many of us have not had a salesperson, usually two weeks before the end of the quarter, explain that if we only add this one feature to the product right now, he or she can close a really, really big deal. Sometimes it's the engineer who prefers to use a new unproven technology rather than the tried and true methods that offer no new personal learning, or add an unneeded feature because it is "cool." Never mind if these decisions make strategic sense for the product. And never mind the impact on overall schedules, risks, existing commitments, launch plans, or any of those other annoying product management issues. But customers don't care about features or technology. **They care only about the benefits that they receive from using your product**. And they vote with their wallets.

It's very common nowadays to make these decisions together with the "development team" or "the sales group." However, that process will often lead to sub-optimal results, **from the viewpoint of the business as a whole**. My manager once asked me to figure out why another product in our group, which was not my responsibility, was getting zero traction in the marketplace. Apparently the highest priority for the product manager was getting "approval" from the engineers on that project, because he never questioned anything. Very quickly, I discovered that the entire design of this product was contrary to the needs of the target customers, so they all rejected it. I needed to make the hard recommendation to kill the project and spare my company the cost of further development and the embarrassment of launching a dead-on-arrival product.

If you permit the "team" or the "group" to vote on key product management decisions, or if you make decisions based on your personal need for "approval" or "respect," you are abdicating your professional responsibilities. **If you are not comfortable providing leadership and making the key decisions, you should step down as product manager in favor of someone who is willing and capable.**

Does the responsibility to make decisions and recommendations mean that you can simply issue edicts from on high? Of course not. Product management, at its best, is a synthesis role. You need to work with other members of your team to make trade-offs and compromises. The key is that these decisions must be based on business needs and objective market realities, not on personalities or the desire to "go along."

30 Agility Is Key to Product Management Success

Matthew Bookspan, Director of Product Management, Voxeo

The two overarching elements for ensuring success are being flexible and having organizational agility.

Many people in our field admit one thing openly: product management is a tough yet very fulfilling job. As a project manager, you serve many masters and have little authority. This can pose challenges, although there are ways to be successful with very little effort on your part.

The two overarching elements for ensuring success are being flexible and having organizational agility. Let's talk more about these two.

So, What Is Flexibility?

I tend to find that those who can change course easily given a specific (or vague) set of parameters can leverage this flexibility for their product's advantage.

However, being flexible doesn't mean caving in to every demand from your respective constituents. Customers, executives, and team members will always demand more of you as they have their respective agendas to fulfill. Thus, know when to flex and when to be firm.

How Do I Discern the Difference between Flexing and Firming?

If there is a primary strength in being flexible, it is the ability to proactively listen and adjust. Being a great product manager means listening without formulating a response prior to the conversation ending. It's echoing back what you've heard so that both (or many) of you are on the same page. Only then are you able to better manage the situation and direct the team to a reasonable answer or conclusion.

Lastly, please note that there is a difference between being flexible and living with ambiguity. The former is about not becoming entrenched in your own beliefs. The latter is about trying to form clarity out of chaos. So, make sure that you understand the difference and that you behave accordingly in the respective situation.

You've Walked Me Through Being Flexible; Now Tell Me about Organizational Agility!

Many factors come into play when managing organizational agility. Some pretty straightforward items include: company size, company culture, where you fit into the org chart and how you view your role within the organization (separate from the org chart itself).

The Basics

You will always have stakeholders making demands of you, and you will most certainly require executive buy-in to move your initiatives forward. However, you also need to know who the other key players in the company are.

It could be a support engineer. It could also be someone in the finance department. It most certainly is any administrative assistant, for, without them, nothing can really get done. Regardless, any one of these people can either help you succeed or fail.

In small to medium organizations, process management can become the biggest challenge. These companies generally are in a new phase of development. It isn't just about the players anymore; it's about how you all work together in an efficient manner.

As you move into larger organizations, the dependency chain becomes more diverse and your ability to grow a personal/social network of key players is crucial to making progress on your deliverables. Here, cross-divisional or cross-departmental goals don't always align, so make sure to have friends in the right places (or have friends of friends).

Going downstream, the final challenge is the startup. Here, there are so few people that ensuring you have strong bonds across all team members is fundamental to success. If the product manager in this type of organization doesn't have respect, then the outcome is usually pretty dire: no more product manager.

Wrapping Up

From the department of redundancy department: being flexible and understanding your organization's specific requirements are key to being a successful product manager.

Understand that flexibility and organizational agility are evolving capabilities. Make sure to grow them wisely and learn from your experiences. And don't forget to have fun too!

31

Tap Into Your Customers

Jen Berkley, Founder, The Insight Advantage

Your *customer's* perceptions are the only thing that matters when it comes to them plunking down money to buy your products.

When I was a product manager managing an entire product line, my instincts told me that our customers held insights that were important to constantly tap into in order to make the best decisions about product features, packaging, marketing messaging, and more.

Now that I'm doing customer research for organizations as a consultant, I'm even more aware of the need to make sure that you integrate your customers' perspective into the design and marketing of products to ensure market success.

How many products do you use that are missing some key feature that would have made the difference between "good" and "great?" How many times do you install new software and think, "I wonder if they tested this on anyone?"

Unfortunately, way too many product development teams are focused on the cool, latest new technology that they want to put in their customers' hands vs. talking to those same customers and understanding things from their perspective. It is common sense—it really doesn't matter what **you** think about your products. What matters is what the buyer and/or user think. And it's all about their perception of how well your products meet their needs. Have you heard the term "perception is reality?" Well, your **customers'** perceptions are the only thing that matters when it comes to them plunking down money to buy your products.

Sure, some people buy products simply because they "need" to have the latest technology. But most of us buy a product because it solves a need or takes away some pain that we are having. So you need to make sure that your products are solving your customers' needs better than your competitors' products are—and that you are communicating that in a way that they can make that connection themselves.

Grant Thornton International Ltd., one of the world's leading organizations of independently owned and managed accounting and consulting firms, published a report in September 2009 ("Innovation: The Key to Future Success?") that explored the sources of innovation. They found that customers are now the leading source of innovations globally (41 percent) and are more important than other sources inside companies, including research and development.

They also found that Asia Pacific organizations are more likely to integrate customer ideas, 48 percent—versus 40 percent of Western European companies and 35 percent of North American companies.

Some of the ways that you can easily integrate customers' perspectives into your product work include:

- Conduct interviews with people from your target market to help you prioritize product features in new products based on what they consider most valuable.
- Conduct ongoing customer surveys to gather current user input that can help you target what changes will be made to future product releases.
- Test your marketing messages out on target customers to see which are most effective.

Make sure to build these types of activities into your product development and launch time line/budget. You may run into resistance based on time, money, and the old engineering argument, "How can customers understand emerging technology?" However, these objections can be overcome.

It doesn't have to take a lot of time and money to make sure that you are launching really great products. Doing so is a great investment that will ensure that you are building something that your customers will really want!

32

Determine Your Marketing Approach Early and Wisely

Barbara Rice, Senior Principal Consultant, 280 Group

A brilliant product without the right marketing approach to support it can result in company failure.

As product managers, you always have to struggle to meet customer needs in the context of an unrealistic schedule in order for the company to meet its objectives. It's easy to get caught up and overwhelmed with turning out a perfect product. But a brilliant product without the right marketing approach to support it can also result in a company failure. Determine your marketing approach early—at least twelve months prior to launch—and you will avoid wasted energy, course correction, and effort with no return. It's the difference between "product readiness" and "market readiness."

Here are some common mistakes companies make when determining the right marketing approach:

- They try to do everything possible in order to create maximum buzz. This is also known as "spray gun marketing," and the basic misconception is that the more marketing you do, the more successful your product will be, even if the marketing efforts are unfocused. You may find you've spent lots of money for mediocre results, or that your team is trying to think "big" but not critically.
- They do what's easy and cheap. This is easy to fall into when finances are tight, and top management may applaud you for making "the tough decisions," but if you follow it, you'll still waste precious marketing budget. It's not only a matter of what you can afford—but finding the right marketing strategies that will be transformational for your product.

- They focus on the kinds of programs the management team loves. Maybe they love PR because they're pumped by industry kudos, or maybe they're fascinated by social media because they want their company to be leading edge and hip. The problem with these pet programs is that while they may stimulate interest or activity, they may not be most effective in reaching your audience.

So what's the best way to avoid these critical errors, and get marketing on the right path early on? While it will likely take many planning sessions to come up with the best marketing mix, here are a few questions that can lead you in the right direction, keep you grounded in reality, and optimize marketing efficiency:

- What (or who) influences your customer the most? Is it other people (industry influencers, colleagues, friends), certain publications or news sources, evidence or proof that your product works? Identifying the "sweet spot" helps ensure your message is on point, and that it's coming from a credible source.
- Are people ready for the "whole product," or do they need to try before they buy? It may be that you want to test different offerings or packages to find out what lowers the barrier to entry.
- What drives your audience to buy? In other words, are they viral, aspirational, data-oriented, etc.? Make sure your message and communication channels support this.
- What is your company's current brand image, and how much latitude do you have with marketing programs? Always be sure your marketing is consistent with this. Don't do a social media program just because someone thinks it's cool; if it's not consistent with your company personality it will almost certainly **not** be cool, and it probably won't have any impact anyway.
- What metrics does your company need to see in order to deem your product a success? Remember that metrics can mean anything from industry buzz to blog pick up to homepage clicks to sales conversions. But don't overlook profitability! Be sure you have a healthy mix of programs that indicate people are moving through the sales cycle.

Overall, make sure you get alignment on your marketing approach **early** —before you dive into the detailed marketing mix. It will go a long way to save time and ensure success. And if you go through your marketing approach early enough, you might find that your product may need some changes itself.

Rule

33 Let the Customer End the Debate

Noël Adams, President, Clearworks

Product managers need a way to stop the debate—a way to provide proof and evidence that the product recommendations they support are the right approach.

One of the biggest challenges (and opportunities) of being a product manager is moderating the internal debate around what the product should "be"—i.e., what it should look like, what features should be included, what functionality is important, etc. You spend endless hours with your engineering team telling you why all the cool things they can build should be included in the product. Sales teams lobby for what they believe is needed for the product to sell. Your CEO probably even chimes in with his/her own great new feature idea. You find yourself agreeing with and even welcoming some of the recommendations, but disagreeing with many others. You base your side of the debate on your market knowledge and your customer-focused approach; meanwhile, all your stakeholders continue to persist that their thinking is correct. You often find yourself in a stalemate, at your wits end thinking about time lines that are being pushed out and budgets that are being over-run. You are left wondering whether you'll even have a product to take to market.

Product managers need a way to stop the debate—a way to provide proof and evidence that the product recommendations they support are the right approach. Product managers need the customer. Successful product managers don't argue their own position on what the product should be. Instead, they present a point and support it with real live customer insights and feedback.

I learned the hard way that the best way to stop the arguing is to present the customer's viewpoint, not my personal viewpoint. Early in my product management career, I battled the engineering team without being armed with the right data, and I lost.

The product unfortunately got launched with those "cool features" I had argued against, and internal teams were left wondering why customers were confused about how to use the product. As a product manager, I didn't wonder why products weren't meeting customer needs. I wondered why I hadn't been able to convince my internal team to support my recommendations.

And that's when I learned the value of arming myself with real customer feedback from solid market research. I learned that customer research generates not only good, unexpected insights for your product throughout the lifecycle, but also provides the tool you need to garner support from your team and other stakeholders—the tool you need to win debates.

Later in my career when engineering questioned me about certain requirements, I pointed to focus groups that I had conducted to gather requirements. When sales asked why we wouldn't include a certain function, I pointed to our customer interviews. And so on. The result was the debate stopped. If you think about it, it makes sense. After all, we aren't building products for ourselves; we're building them for customers. We can't speak for customers. They have to speak for themselves.

There are a lot of great reasons to get customer input. As a good product manager, inherently you understand the value of talking to the customer. However, it's important to remember to use that feedback to manage the internal discussions and debates. Doing so will alleviate many headaches and deliver a better product.

34 Differentiation Isn't Enough, You Have to Be Better

Paul Alexander Gray, Consultant, brainmates pty ltd

Differentiation is not enough. Discover how effective product managers are winning by making their products "better."

In an environment of product proliferation and intense competition, product managers must do more than just differentiate. They must find ways to satisfy customer needs and wants in ways that are 'better' than competitive offerings.

Consider the case of hotel accommodation—a market crammed with competitive offerings that differ in pricing, amenities, location, service, and other more intangible factors. It's not only competitors that seek to differentiate their products, but brands within a company as well. The Hilton Hotel family consists of no less than nine brands from Hampton Inn to Waldorf Astoria Resorts.

Customers are faced with an almost overwhelming choice. How do products differ? In what ways are they similar? Which one is the best product for me?

The concept of differentiation seeks to identify and highlight ways in which one product is different than others. The desired outcome is an understanding or recognition within your target audience that your product is different from competitor offerings.

Product managers need to go one step further. It's not enough to be perceived as different. Successful differentiation requires that products stand out from competitive offerings by providing the greatest value to the customer. Product managers need to look at three areas:

- **What customers want:** Understand the problems before you design the solution. It's important to hone in on your target audience and get to know what specific problems they are experiencing. What are the impacts of these problems? What would happen if the problems were removed? What would need to happen to reduce or remove this problem?

- **What you're good at:** There may be plenty of valid problems out there in your target audience but these are irrelevant if you're not able to solve these. There are plenty of examples of brands diversifying into new territory only to fail because they lacked the core competencies to be able to satisfy customer needs and wants. Do what you're good at.
- **Where competitors are weak:** Even if you have identified valid problems and know that you have the ability to solve these, it won't matter much if you're entering a crowded marketplace where multiple competitors can do the exact same thing.

The intersection of these three areas is the best opportunity for going beyond differentiation to define, develop and deploy a product that is more likely to succeed.

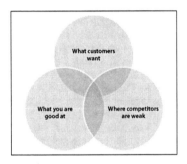

In our hotel context, let's look at very price sensitive, solo travelers in their mid-twenties. They might have grown out of sleeping in noisy youth hostels but not have the money or interest in splashing cash out on a fancy room. Our segment wants a bare-bones room—literally a bed and a shower for as little money as possible. This frees up their money to spend on eating out, hitting the bars, or going sightseeing.

EasyHotel[ix] offers a service for this segment. Their spartan rooms consist of a bed, a TV, and an en suite bathroom. No desk, chair, phone, mini-bar, gym, or pool. Rooms are not cleaned every day. It's not all bad though. Their hotels are well located in places where tourists want to stay, and they're incredibly cheap.

Few competitors can match EasyHotel's offerings. Even budget chains of major brands have more frills and a higher price point. Youth hostels, B&B's and independent hotels can't match its consistent quality and model. EasyHotel's proposition of low price with basic but consistent quality is doing well with new properties opening in Germany and Spain in 2010.

Successful differentiation depends on understanding your target market segment needs, defining solutions based on your ability to satisfy these needs, and developing and deploying products that meet these needs in ways that provide more value than competitors.

Act Like a Child

**Michaela Zwinakis, VP of
Solution Management, Governance Risk,
and Compliance Solutions, SAP**

One of the most important skills a product manager can adopt is as simple as remembering how to act like a child.

One of the key responsibilities of a product manager is to determine underlying customer needs or problems. Once they are identified, the work begins to design and market a better solution. However, the skill required to get to these underlying needs is often overlooked. Many product managers, and even product management courses, teach you to interview the customer, exploring what it is they would like to see in a solution or how they would best like to get their job done. However, many of these techniques overlook the key to uncovering the real problem for which the customer needs a solution. That is, what it is that is fundamentally "broken" for the customer and needs to be addressed. In customer interaction scenarios, one of the best methods to get to this underlying information is to act like a child and continue to ask "Why?" until you reach a thorough understanding of the customer need or problem.

Most sentient beings have had an interaction with a two-, three-, or four-year-old that goes something like this: You say, "We need to get ready to go home now" (or some such directive), and the child replies, "Why?" You then patiently explain the day's schedule and why it is important to go home now, and how this causally ties in with the rest of the day's plans. The child simply responds "Why?" You may or may not now respond as patiently, explaining why these plans were set, to which the child will respond in turn, "Why?" This pattern then repeats *ad nauseam* until one or both of you give up in utter frustration or abruptly end the conversation with an emphatic "I don't know."

While sometimes frustrating, it turns out children are learning. In fact, while these questions may be repetitious to a painful degree, the key is that the child is engaging in a deeper learning exchange. Interestingly, researchers have lately found the strongest learning environments are the ones in which adults engage in rich conversations with children in just such environments (interestingly, even with those as young as two years old).[x]

Product management is no different. That is, in order to have the greatest learning, it is important to have a series of rich conversations with your customer. One of the basic techniques I have found to be most successful is to act like a child and continue to ask "Why?" I often counsel product managers to then repeat this until they truly feel that they have exhausted the topic and have a deep understanding of the specific issue the customer is trying to solve.

So, when a customer asks you for a specific feature or answers your question about how they perform this task daily or how they would want to, ask them "Why?" Carefully listen to their answer, understand it, and then ask them "Why?" again. The goal is to drill down to the underlying causes of the behavior. What is the key problem they are trying to solve? It is important to point out that this technique is most successfully employed by carefully adjusting your tone with each "Why?" to explicitly **not** sound like a child. But ask the question again, each time you have gained an understanding of what your customer has just told you.

I can guarantee that if you stop with the first "Why?" you are likely to design a solution that misses the mark. You will be solving for a very specific problem that may not generalize well or may not truly represent the actual problem they are trying to solve. By asking why again and again, you uncover the root cause or the base level need. By getting to this level, you will then have many more degrees of freedom in designing an appropriate solution and, in the end, I can guarantee you will have a delighted customer.

36

Decide What You Are Going to Do and Not Do

Mike Freier, Senior Principal Consultant, 280 Group

Companies must also be clear about what businesses and market segments they are not going to support because every company has limited resources.

Regardless of size, every company has limited resources and must make some tough decisions about what product and services they want to offer. In parallel, companies must also decide what market segments they are not going to pursue at any given point in time. When companies understand the nuances of markets, they are able to build winning products and solutions, increase sales revenue, and have the capital for sustained growth.

Let's take a closer look at why it's important to understand market segments.

Large markets represent billions (or trillions) of dollars of opportunity. But they cannot be approached at this level because large markets are really a composite of medium markets which are made up of smaller and smaller markets. Each market segment supports a specific group of market needs.

Markets	Automotive Market
Automotive	Emerging (Electric/Hybrid Vehicles)
Banking/Finance	Exotic (Porsche, Ferrari, Maserati)
Energy	High-End (Mercedes Benz, BMW, Lexus)
Software	Mid-Range (Honda Accord, Toyota Camry)
Telecommunications	Low-End (Kia Rio, Toyota Yarus, etc.)

Figure: Sample Markets and Automotive Market Segments

Further Market Segmentation Techniques

As markets mature, companies need to put more energy into positioning and choose those market segments which best align with their products, services, and solutions offering as well as core competencies. In general, companies that position at the high end of a market are not able to also sell products at the low end. Likewise, high-fashion brands are not appealing to no-frills utilitarian buyers and high-fashion brand buyers prefer the brand because of its exclusivity and would not purchase a mainstream product.

New and adjacent markets can also represent growth opportunities for companies, but need to be looked at strategically because supporting a new business requires dedicated resources and capital.

So, Does (Company) Size Matter?

Early stage and small companies must identify a market problem and build their product/solution around this need. Picking an initial market segment is critical for success because a one-size-fits-all solution is not practical to build and probably not compelling to anyone.

For example, Tesla Motors entered the saturated car market with a $100,000 electric roadster, which is a niche market segment for sport car enthusiasts. This high-end entry point allowed Tesla to develop and prove out new technology while generating some revenue and working on their second-generation car, a four-door luxury sedan designed for the high-end market.

In contrast, larger companies support multiple market segments and must be clear about their core business solutions. As companies grow, the cost to support multiple product lines and market segments also increases. Broader products/solutions also add complexity to the buying process. Tesla, for example, has two car models while BMW has over fifty.

Deciding What Not to Do

Companies must also be clear about what businesses and market segments they are not going to support because every company has limited resources.

Companies should look at the size and growth of markets, their current offerings, technical expertise, and competition to strategically decide where to apply resources to get the **largest** return on their investment.

Deciding what not to do is a natural fallout of their current product and business plans and may be parsed into three groups. First, if a market segment is clearly outside a company's domain expertise, it's easy to discount. Second, if the company is resource constrained and wants to pursue an adjacent market segment, the opportunity may become a road map item. And to close, after reviewing and prioritizing all the market/product opportunities, a company may decide to put some projects on hold and revisit the opportunity in six to twelve-plus months.

37

Trust and Leadership Through Good Relationships

Howard Rosenfield, Founder and Principal Consultant, Matanzas Creek Consulting, LLC

All of these necessary skills are wasted without the ability to motivate and lead the broader team to achieve a common goal.

Product management is both a challenging and rewarding job. The former stems largely from the fact that as product managers we have a great deal of the responsibility, but little direct authority to achieve the desired result. The latter can be realized by overcoming the challenges through the establishment of trust and leadership.

In the product delivery process, each team member has a well-defined skill set that is oriented at delivering a result within the functional domain—technical writers produce product documentation, software engineers develop software by writing code, and so on. Product management is different in that its purpose is to work across functions and ensure that everyone is delivering the necessary ingredients to build a whole product that will resonate with the market. To be sure, other skills are required—multitasking, rapid assimilation and processing of facts, and the ability to make decisions are but a few. However, all of these necessary skills are wasted without the ability to motivate and lead the broader team to achieve a common goal.

When engaging in a project as the "new product manager," I frequently find that there is an initial level of apprehension on the part of some extended team members. This may be partly a result of having worked with an ineffective product manager in the past. Undoubtedly, the team's trepidation also stems from standard group dynamics where the assumption is that someone from outside of a given functional domain is working against the interests of that group. A good product manager will transcend this adversarial reflex by gaining the trust of all extended team members, regardless of role.

So, how does this magic happen? Well, it begins with treating everyone with respect and camaraderie. This may sound trite, but a visit to someone's desk to just say "hello" and ask them about their weekend or what they're working on because you are curious and interested can go a long way to establishing that you're "OK." I find that a casual visit with no agenda is so unusual in most high-pressure environments that it can begin establishing trust by the sheer nature of its contrast to the norm. You may not end up being everyone's best friend—product management is also about managing conflict, after all—but the team members will gain a sense of trust that you are working with them and not against them.

Beyond building positive one-on-one relationships, the effective product manager must also demonstrate leadership across the cross-functional team. To be sure, many books have been written on the subject so it is impossible to capture everything in a single essay. However, at the core of all leadership is communication.

As a product manager, you should take the initiative in establishing and leading regular team meetings so that all extended team members can articulate what they're working on, hear what others are doing, and identify dependencies and areas for collaboration. Use this forum to encourage cooperation and remind the team what the overarching product vision is in order to avoid "forest and trees" derailments and keep everyone on target. Establishing yourself as a leader by promoting communication will help you to motivate the team without any direct authority.

By approaching team members as fellow human beings and helping to foster communication, you can establish trust and lead the team to effectively ship products—and have some fun at the same time. To quote an old TV commercial, "Try it, you'll like it!"

Great Execution Trumps a Great Product Idea

Janet George, Director of
Research Engineering, Yahoo! Research

A good product idea with great execution can be worth $200 million. A brilliant idea with mediocre execution is worth about $20.

Focusing on execution is often challenging, especially for product managers, because there are thousands of little decisions that need to be made when bringing a new product to market. These decisions can be broadly classified into four categories:

1. Market, customer, product, and functionality
2. Sales and distribution
3. Usability
4. Technical, engineering, implementation, maintenance, and support

Category 1: Market, Customer, Product, and Functionality

Product managers are only experts in the first area but have to drive decision making in all four categories. They must resist taking the path of least resistance offered by the loudest, most political, or powerful stakeholders. Although expedient, this will not yield the best decisions. Instead, the product manager must seek out the low-key experts in each area to ensure optimal decisions.

So what are some of the hurdles in these broad categories? And how does a good product manager overcome them without losing sight of the market requirements and the ultimate goals for the product?

Category 2: Distribution

How does one make the right product execution decision when market requirements conflict with the distribution requirements? Which one takes precedence? For example, if the distribution of the product or the application is through iPhones but the target market customers do not use iPhones, do you execute the product for the target market and then try to figure out how to get the product in the hands of your customer? Or do you go after the iPhone users—in other words, develop for the distribution channel without focus of the target market and demographics of the customers in the target market? These are complex decisions, and thorough market and competitive research is necessary. The work must be conducted without bias.

Category 3: Usability

Great technology and sometimes great functionality can be highly unusable. Focusing on one without the other will lead to mediocre products that are either too hard to use or too limited in their functionality. Instead, focus on great usability with great functionality to create the "wow" experiences that will set the product idea and concept far above the competition. The product manager's goal here is to make decisions that focus on actual usability with great functionality. Stay away from cool designer touches and a fancy, eye-popping, flashy look and feel without ease of use. Likewise, sort out conflicting marketing and usability requirements.

Category 4: Technical, Engineering, Implementation, Support, and Maintenance

Derived technical requirements, including performance, systems, hardware, infrastructure, load balancing, and scalability, are all really hard to uncover in full depth at the early stages of requirement analysis because these usually have embedded dependencies. As implementation proceeds through nested dependencies, new technical requirements emerge. Often this occurs late in the execution stage making the matters more challenging and urgent.

To overcome these problems, the good product manager must understand from where the derived requirements stem and solicit a good evaluation of trade-offs and downsides from experts in specific technical areas. Cost factors must also be fully considered. Surprises in cost can turn a money-maker into a money loser and sink a project.

Great execution is all about establishing the right requirements and goals for the product. The entire product's success and return on development investment depends on it. A simple example illustrates this point. Consider the goal of "sending a man to the moon" versus "sending a man to the moon and bringing him back alive." These two similar goals would lead a team to different conclusions and design decisions. In the first case, it only matters that the man makes it to the moon for the project team to claim victory. In the second case, the project would be deemed a failure if the man made it to the moon but was not returned safely to Earth. It is, therefore, critically important to get the product requirements, spanning all broad categories, right for the team to successfully execute on the product.

39 Be All You Can Be

Reena Kapoor, Founder and Chief Strategist, Conifer Consulting

Think like a general manager.

Product management is a unique, central, powerful function when structured properly. You have all the responsibility but may feel like you have no authority. But you do have something very powerful at your disposal—influence. When a question arises about product direction, all eyes turn to you. If that's not happening, ask yourself if you're being a true product leader. You can—and should—be a key influencer in your company. But for that you need to think like a general manager—not merely a product manager.

What does this mean? A general manager (GM) is a manager of the business, usually responsible for all aspects of the business including the P&L (profit and loss) and revenue and growth goals. Note the "L" of P/L means you have to think about not just growing the business but also the cost and operations side. While this might seem like a lofty goal when all that you're thinking about is getting the requirements defined, it will greatly increase your chances of success to think like a GM vs. merely a PM. Take the time to step back and think about the overall context for your product. Here are a few categories of thoughts to consider:

- **Market dynamics:** What is the market you're in or entering? Is it a new category you're creating or is it an existing one? Is it growing, stagnant, or declining? What impact will your (new) product have on the market?
- **Customer and share of market:** Who are your target customers and who are your competitors? Think about both direct, obvious competitors as well as what other options and substitutes exist for the customer. If they don't choose you, why

not? Given what emerges from this question, you might also consider how you differentiate your offering. And finally, what kind of market share do you expect to capture? How?

- **Business model:** Why will customers or other stakeholders pay for the benefits your product/service provides or ancillary value it creates? What's your business model or how will you make money?
- **Pricing and value:** What will you charge for your services? If your offering is "free" to customers, do you have a "premium" offering in mind and/or are you selling ancillary offerings to other stakeholders (e.g., targeted ads, virtual goods, etc.)? What's your planned margin structure? What cannibalization can you expect from your new product among your existing ones?
- **Total customer experience and operational impact:** One of the great promises we ask product managers to deliver on is "How to deliver on an excellent total experience at every customer touchpoint?" While this is a worthy goal and a fruitful exercise, what gets left out is the answer to the following question: "What will it take operationally for the organization to deliver on this promise?" Is your organization set up for this? If you build it, they might come, but will they stay? The answer might depend on how easy it was for them to "buy" what's right for them and use it, and even the after-sales experience.
- **Product life-cycle management:** Is there a natural life cycle for your product? Is there an industry/strategic/technological inflection point coming? Do you have a plan for making your offering obsolete—before the market does?

While fulfilling the above is a tall order, even being aware of these questions, bringing them to the table, and showing your team why this matters is a great first step. Be sure to ask these questions and engage actively in discussions and decisions before the fate of your product is sealed. You may not be the person with the authority to solve all these problems but you will be seen as a leader and a key influencer if you're raising them, seeking the sources for answers, and collaborating in multi-functional teams to make sure these are being addressed.

40

I Can See Clearly Now: The Power of Transparency

Christine Crandell, Senior Vice President
of Global Marketing, Accept Software

By helping, you tap into a vast pool of knowledge that would not otherwise be available; a fully transparent development process brings a number of important advantages.

Product creation and enhancement has evolved into a high-speed, market-driven undertaking. Product makers are becoming leaner and more agile in their approaches to product development as well as in other facets of their business. And during the past few years, their pace of innovation has accelerated into a steady drumbeat of incremental innovations and refinements involving multiple iterations and numerous stakeholders.

Keeping on top of the constant stream of ideas—weighing them, balancing them, prioritizing them, and eventually integrating them—is a task that no individual or product management team can do alone. Indeed, a product manager's greatest fear today is overlooking, and as a result missing, a requirement that provides a key competitive advantage. Misunderstandings, conflicts, and lost opportunities occur routinely because, without a comprehensive view of the process, members on the same team can end up working at cross-purposes, to the frustration of everyone in the organization—especially its C-level executives. It is a problem exacerbated by changing market conditions including shorter product cycles, higher customer expectations, and more intense competition.

Linking together stakeholders so that everyone has access to the same information at the same time is the essence of transparency. Creating the opportunity for that to happen involves building a central repository for ideas, suggestions, requirements, and the comments associated with them—a single source of truth that everyone in the process can see. It involves providing stakeholders, both within and outside the organization, access to as much of that information as possible and the ability to collaborate on that information across every life cycle phase of the company's product line.

Naturally, people who are asked for their input insist that they want what they want. But whenever the basis for a requirements decision is made transparent to everyone who has a stake in the outcome, people tend to accept the result—even if it's not the one they had hoped for. Where they can see for themselves and understand the reasons supporting a decision, the potential for negative reactions is greatly diminished.

By helping you tap into a vast pool of knowledge that would not otherwise be available, a fully transparent development process brings a number of important advantages to the task of defining the right product for the right market at the right time. But it also requires accepting a greater degree of flexibility—including greater latitude in setting timetables—and the recognition that some of what you attempt may not pan out. Even then, however, a transparent process gives you the opportunity to fail early rather than late. It's faster, better, and a whole lot cheaper to get feedback early and then change course.

For the producer of any product, it is far better to discover early on that the direction in which they're going is not the right one than it is to go through a full development cycle only to find out in the marketplace that they were wrong.

Transparency offers a gut check, a feedback loop, a backup for the product manager's instincts, which can become overwhelmed by the surge of requirements that an active community of stakeholders is capable of generating. That enables you faster time to market with less rework, and makes you better able to hit the target on the first pass as a result of the extensive upfront input and validation. Cost of development, as a result, is lower and the return on development investment increases dramatically. Competitive advantages also flow from being faster to market with the right products. And your customers, in turn, claim greater satisfaction with the products they receive.

41

Always Be Learning

**Therese Padilla, Co-Founder
and President, AIPMM**

Product managers are considered "know-it-alls." Make sure you are worthy of the title.

"I never teach my pupils; I only attempt to provide the conditions in which they can learn."
– Albert Einstein

In the 1965 article, "Cramming More Components onto Integrated Circuits," Gordon E. Moore explained that components in a circuit would increase in capacity by 200 percent per year, or, in other words, we can get a whole lot of stuff on a little wafer. He went on to say that there was no predictable end in that trend. This concept went on to become known as Moore's Law. Being the pragmatist that I am, I saw no reason to doubt this law. It was at that moment of embracing Moore's Law as truth, that I knew I would spend every day of my adult life learning.

Keeping current in all trends—technology, business, industry, political, culture—requires a passionate desire to study. The most successful product managers I have known were as comfortable reading Michael Crichton as they were reading *Applied Economics*. In fact, they spent much of their time in between meetings reading the latest analyst reports and marking up the margins with notes.

I now have the great fortune of working with some of the greatest product managers in the world, and the reason I meet them is because they have a great passion to learn more about their profession; they are hungry for knowledge. You could say they are "cramming more components onto the integrated circuits" of their brains.

Here are the steps to successful lifetime learning:

- Learn from others—your teammates are a wealth of knowledge. In your team you have engineers, scientists, researchers, marketers, sales and customer service representatives. Each of these individuals can teach you about their area of expertise. Look at them as an untapped resource.
- Learn the disciplines that complement your skills—in your capacity as a product manager you touch a multitude of business disciplines. Take the time to learn about each of these disciplines. Don't be hands off on topics that were not in your major. If you don't know anything about finance, take an online course on finance for non-financial managers. Do you spend your time immersed in technology? Take a marketing course at your local college. You will be surprised at what you will be able to apply instantly to your career.
- Learn your industry and expand to other industries—being a master of your industry requires continual learning. No industry is static, and growth is happening all around you. Another way to learn is to contrast. By learning other industries, you gain an advantage of contrasting your industry, and it will help you see things you might have missed. This is the holistic versus myopic view of the industry.
- Learn from the obvious—as a product manager, you probably think you don't have anything else you need to learn about product management. You can surround yourself with a group of experts by taking a class, attending a seminar, listening to a webinar, or attending a conference.

Learning is a journey with no final destination. In Moore's wisdom, he pointed out that capacity was increasing and we couldn't assume the status quo. The same is true for product managers who have to keep up with an ever-expanding horizon. Product managers are considered "know-it-alls." Make sure you are worthy of the title.

•

•

42

These Are Our Rules. What Are Yours?

Greg Cohen, Senior
Principal Consultant, 280 Group

As we look to advance our products, we must be aware of the larger picture and environment in which we work.

Rules are designed to prevent failure and, in particular, the repetition of failure. The majority of rules in the book emerged from the personal, observed, or near failures of each rule's author in bringing a successful product to market. It is therefore worth reflecting on the fact that this seemingly concise book of 42 Rules contains over five centuries of collected wisdom from the contributors, and many of these lessons were learned from the school of hard knocks.

If you were searching for the grand unified theory of physics, forty-two might seem like a large number. But in the much more complex world of product management, forty-two is relatively small—enough to capture the essence of the topic, but not to cover every situation you will encounter in your career. Therefore, each day we must ask what we can do to make our products more successful. The rules contained in this book can help by provoking you to think differently about how you do your job and manage your products. But this book, or any other book for that matter, does not contain all the answers, nor does it contain the nonexistent single formula for success.

As we look to advance our products, we must be aware of the larger picture and environment in which we work. Do we understand our customers? Do we understand how they perceive value? Does our team know this as well? Is there a solution that our company is capable of delivering, and have we persuaded management to invest in this opportunity? Through this endeavor, we each create our own rules of what works, what doesn't, and what can be improved.

Further, as stated in Rule 1: Rules Are Meant to Be Broken. The art is in knowing which rule to break, when to break it, and why to break it. For this, unfortunately, there is no rule. It is our hope, however, that the reader will have the insight to know when to apply a rule, the courage to know when to reinvent it, and the wisdom to know the difference.

It is your turn now to add to the body of knowledge, to test new theories, and to identify patterns of success and patterns of failure. What is your rule? We would love to hear from you. Email us at: 42rules@280group.com.

A Contributing Authors

Adams, Noël

Noël Adams is President of Clearworks (http://www.clearworks.net), where she and her team of product experts help clients define and launch new products and services integrating customer insights and user research from idea through launch. The team has worked with large and small companies in both the consumer and business space across a variety of industries.

Berkley, Jen

Jen Berkley is the Owner of The Insight Advantage (http://www.theinsightadvantage.com), which provides organizations with research services, helping gather customer insights and integrate those insights into product development/product management efforts.

Bookspan, Matthew

With twenty years of experience and having shipped over forty software products, Bookspan has a keen understanding of how to make products successful. As a product manager, he believes in agility, leanness, and consensus building. Throughout his career, he has had the privilege of working for Apple, Microsoft, Cisco, Electronic Arts, and more.
(http://www.linkedin.com/in/mbookspan)

Burton, Phil

Phil Burton, Senior Principal Consultant and Trainer, joined 280 Group in 2007 after a twenty-five-plus-year product management and product marketing career in both established companies and startups, focused on information security, data communications, and networking. His expertise is in product life cycle management with a focus on customizing the process to the specific needs and organizational structure of a company.

Cagan, Marty

Marty Cagan is the Founder of The Silicon Valley Product Group (http://www.svpg.com) and is the author of the book *Inspired: How To Create Products Customers Love*. Marty is a Silicon Valley-based product executive with more than 20 years of experience with industry leaders including eBay, America Online, Netscape Communications and Hewlett-Packard. Before founding SVPG to pursue his interests in helping others create successful products through his writing, speaking, consulting and training, Marty was most recently Senior Vice-President of Product Management and Design for eBay.

Chalif, Ivan

Ivan Chalif is a product management and product marketing professional with more than a decade of experience successfully launching and managing web-based applications for both SaaS and onsite use. Ivan shares his knowledge and experiences in product management (and, occasionally, a bad pun or two) on his blog, The Productologist (http://www.theproductologist.com/).

Cook, John

John Cook has been a consultant and an executive in product marketing for almost twenty years. He has held senior-level product management and marketing positions in many high-tech companies including Apple, Palm and HP. John is a left brain/right brain person, who's as comfortable talking with engineers as the customers who buy their products. He enjoys diving under the hood of technology and has a long track record of delivering successful technology products to customers worldwide. He's a hands-on person, who's not afraid to explore and use the products he works with.

Coster, Nick

Nick Coster is a Co-founder of brainmates who is passionate about the benefits of putting the customer before the technology and building products and services that delight the buyer and the user. Nick has been developing and managing products for over thirteen years, with a range of different companies including Telstra BigPond, Excite@Home, Optus, Westpac and eBay, delivering internet service and telecommunications, online applications, and internet security products. In the process of this journey he has developed a deep understanding of the way the different technologies fit together and is always amazed at the new and exciting ways that people use them. http://brainmates.com.au

Crandell, Christine

Christine Crandell has more than twenty years of executive management, marketing, and business development experience in technology and sits on several advisory boards including Coupa and SDForum. She is the Senior Vice President of Global Marketing at Accept Software and is a frequent speaker and writer. Accept Corporation offers online product innovation management software to help technology-driven companies choose the right products for the right markets with the fastest time-to-profit. The Accept360 Suite is the only complete end-to-end software solution that dynamically links company and product strategy with product execution through ideation, portfolio analysis, requirements prioritization, collaboration, dashboard visibility, and real time analytics. For more information, visit:
http://www.accept360.com or call us at 866.423.8376.

Dersh, Dave

As VP of Consulting & Training at the 280 Group, David is responsible for growing the company's overall services business. David joined the 280 Group in early 2008, having served in a variety of sales and account management roles, including: global account manager, business development executive, and territory sales representative. He brings over twenty years of technology sales and business development experience to his roles at the 280 Group. Previously, he worked in various sales, business development, and marketing roles at Sun Microsystems, Intel, and Apple Computer. David holds a BS in Information Systems, from San Diego State University and an MBA from University of California, Irvine.

Dver, Alyssa

Alyssa Dver is the CEO of Mint Green Marketing, and author of both *Software Product Management Essentials* and *No Time Marketing*. In addition to her consulting work, Alyssa does keynote presentations and workshops several times each month at conferences, associations, and corporate meetings. Published in Forbes, BusinessWeek, Entrepreneur, Software Magazine, and dozens more, Alyssa is also frequently interviewed by the likes of BusinessWeek and American Express OPEN for her business success and knowledge. Connect with her at:
http://notimemarketing.com.

Epstein, Kevin

Kevin Epstein is a Silicon Valley executive with two decades of experience leading product management and marketing teams at such software industry highfliers as Netscape, RealNetworks, Inktomi, and VMware. Kevin holds an undergraduate degree in high-energy nuclear physics from Brown University, an MBA from Stanford (where he teaches the occasional course), is the author of *Marketing Made Easy* (Entrepreneur Magazine Press/McGraw Hill), and serves as an outside advisor to various venture-backed and individual entrepreneurial startup companies.

Evans, Tom

Tom Evans is Principal at Lûcrum Marketing and brings over twenty years of successful high-tech business experience helping startups as well as Fortune 500 companies create and launch winning products. He is recognized for building product management and product marketing organizations from the ground up that develop market-driven technology solutions, create compelling go-to-market strategies, and build strategic partnerships that drive revenue growth in the US and global markets.

Fradin, David

David Fradin is a Senior Principal Consultant for the 280 Group. He began his career as a product manager with Hewlett Packard Corporation, followed by product and business unit manager with Apple Computer. Subsequently, he worked as associate director of the Personal Computer Industry Service at Dataquest, vice president of marketing and sales at Docugraphix, president/founder of Desktop Video Products and president/founder of Digital Enterprises Corporation, a leading computer and Web-based training developer. He has been responsible for product management (or, in a more senior role) for bringing to market seventy-plus hardware, software, SaaS, Internet, mobile, and service products that have produced $250-million-plus in revenue.

Freier, Mike

Mike Freier is a Senior Principal Consultant with the 280 Group. He has over twelve years of experience in product marketing and management with a total of twenty-two years of high-tech experience in both hardware and integrated systems software development. During his career, he has defined market and product requirements, researched and identified new vertical markets, developed a suite of sales collateral/tools, and has been responsible for the life cycle of several products. In addition to full-time work, Mike is President of the Silicon Valley Product Management Association (http://www.svpma.org) and serves on the MIT-Stanford VLAB Executive Committee. Mike graduated from the University of Massachusetts at Amherst with a BS in Mechanical Engineering.

Gaeta, Sarah Rosenbaum

At Plastic Logic, Sarah Gaeta's leadership has helped define the content strategy for QUE, the first proReader designed for business professionals. In her role, she is responsible for creating unique reading experiences, managing partner fulfillment, and monitoring circulation and advertising tracking. Prior to joining Plastic Logic, Sarah spent seventeen years at Adobe Systems, where she oversaw strategic and go-to-market planning and execution, competitive analysis, and product vision definition. During her tenure, she helped grow Adobe Acrobat prosumer market share, increased enterprise penetration, drove the establishment of PDF use in print publishing and the first PDF-X standard definition and product line segmentation to address wider market needs.

George, Janet

Janet George is Director of Research Engineering for Yahoo! Research and currently leads the innovative product requirements, design, development, engineering, Infrastructure, implementation, and website teams in Yahoo! Research. She is responsible for all the execution and implementation of breakthrough innovation, building and growing the Research Engineering Organization with professional, scaleable research infrastructure and a world class professional Yahoo! Research and Yahoo! Labs website. Janet is also engaged in building a Research Engineering Organization in Bangalore India with global implementation of the breakthrough innovations.

Prior to Yahoo!, Janet served as senior director for a portfolio of innovative whitespace emerging products and technologies at Intuit; and as vice president at Andale, responsible for leadership and management of the Andale Research Products and User Experience Champion teams. Prior to Andale. Janet held positions at eBay and Etak/Sony, which merged with TeleAtlas. She brings with her a wealth of twenty-plus years of experience garnered at a number of top tier companies like Apple computer, Informix Software, and Hewlett Packard Labs. Janet holds an advanced Master's Degree and BS in Computer Science, Mathematics, and Electronics, with eighteen years of education, solid fundamentals, and training in the field of computer science and software development.

Gorchels, Linda

Linda Gorchels is on the executive education faculty of the Wisconsin School of Business and author of three books, including *The Product Manager's Handbook* and *The Product Manager's Field Guide*.

Gray, Paul

Paul Gray is a consultant with brainmates, an Australian product management and marketing agency. Paul is passionate about infusing creativity and a 'devils advocate' approach to developing products and creating compelling marketing strategies. In his time at brainmates, Paul has conducted competitor and market analysis, developed positioning and segmentation frameworks and devised value propositions for clients in the entertainment, financial services, software, and "not-for-profit" industries. Paul has over ten years of experience in product marketing within media, entertainment, and communications, having worked for leading clients in Europe and Australia including Disney and Foxtel. http://brainmates.com.au

Gray, Paula

Paula Gray is an applied cultural anthropologist at the Association of International Product Marketing & Management.

Hohmann, Luke

Luke Hohmann is the Founder and CEO of The Innovation Games® Company (http://innovationgames.com/), the leading provider of serious games that enable organizations to solve complex problems through online and in-person collaborative play. He's been known to take naps on his SOFA only to find himself covered in stickers when he wakes up.

Kapoor, Reena

Reena Kapoor is the Founder and Chief Strategist at Conifer Consulting (http://www.coniferlnc.com), a product and marketing strategy consulting firm in the Bay Area, since 2005. Reena brings nearly twenty years of new products and brand management experience from Fortune 100 CPG companies and venture-backed Silicon Valley companies. Her deep consumer brand and general management experience stem from tenures at Procter & Gamble and Kraft Foods, where she last ran the $100 million Knudsen brand. Following that, Reena has played leadership product and marketing strategy roles at enterprise software and online consumer marketing services companies. Reena has a B.Tech degree from the Indian Institute of Technology (IIT), New Delhi, and a master's degree from Northwestern University.

Krieps, Mara

Mara Krieps is a Founder of Pivotal Product Management (http://www.pivotalpm.com), a product management consultancy in Seattle, WA. She applies her twenty years of leadership in product management and marketing strategy to help companies and product managers to greater product success. Mara heads the Seattle-based Product Management Consortium (http://www.pmcnw.org). She received AIPMM's "Excellence in Product Management Education" award in 2006, and in 2009 she was named by the Puget Sound Business Journal's TechFlash as one of the "Top 100 Women in Seattle Tech." Mara is an AIPMM Certified Product Manager and Agile Certified Product Manager.

Krock, Eric

Eric Krock is Chief Marketing Officer at a startup that's currently in stealth mode. You can find his blog on product and project management at http://www.voximate.com/. Previously, he was vice president of product at Zvents, director of product management at VeriSign and Kontiki, and group product manager for the Gecko browser engine at Netscape.

Lash, Jeff

Jeff Lash has over ten years of experience in product management and user experience design for online products for companies including Elsevier, MasterCard International, and XPLANE. He blogs about product management at "How To Be A Good Product Manager" (http://www.goodproductmanager.com), runs the product management Q-and-A site "Ask A Good Product Manager" (http://ask.goodproductmanager.com), and dispenses product management wisdom 140 characters at a time on Twitter (twitter.com/jefflash). Jeff lives in St. Louis, MO.

Merrick, Linda

Linda Merrick is a founder of Pivotal Product Management (http://www.pivotalpm.com), a product management consultancy in Seattle, WA. She applies her twenty-five years of leadership in product management to help companies and product managers improve product success. Linda also leads the instructor team for the University of Washington Certificate program in Product Management. She received AIPMM's "Excellence in Product Management Education" award in 2007, and in 2009 was named by the Puget Sound Business Journal's TechFlash as one of the "Top 100 Women in Seattle Tech." Linda is an AIPMM Certified Product Manager and Agile Certified Product Manager.

Mironov, Rich

Rich Mironov is one of Silicon Valley's preeminent experts in technology product management and corporate-focused technical marketing. As an entrepreneur, early-stage employee, and consultant, he has worked at and with dozens of technology companies in Silicon Valley and around the country. Rich pioneered the product management meet-ups now known as P-Camps or Product Camps. He is the author of *The Art of Product Management: Lessons from a Silicon Valley Innovator.* To read further musings or to sign up for Rich's product management newsletter *ProductBytes*, go to: http://www.mironov.com

Moorehead, James

James Morehead joined Support.com (http://support.com) in October 2003 and is currently Vice President of Product Management. James leads a global product management team responsible for the product road map, market research, and detailed requirements for the technology that drives Support.com's premium technology services offering. Support.com services are offered directly to consumers under the Support.com brand and as a white label service via retailers, ISVs, ISPs, and PC-OEMS.

Mueller, Fritz

Fritz Mueller is the Senior Director of Product Management for archiving software and services at i365, a Seagate Company. Prior to i365, Fritz was in charge of product management for several networking and software startups including Keynote Systems, the first Internet performance management service. Fritz has a BS in Computer Engineering from the University of Michigan and an MBA from the University of Chicago.

Olsen, Dan

Dan Olsen is CEO and Co-founder of YourVersion, a real-time discovery engine startup that won the TechCrunch50 People's Choice Award. Dan led product management for Quicken and Friendster and has consulted to many startups. Dan has nineteen years of high-tech experience, engineering degrees from Northwestern and Virginia Tech, and a Stanford MBA. (http://www.olsensolutions.com)

Padilla, Therese

Therese Padilla is Co-founder and President of the Association of International Product Marketing & Management (AIPMM). Therese has a long career working for high-tech companies such as Symantec/Peter Norton Group, Quarterdeck, Command Software and F-Secure.

Reekes, Jim

Jim Reekes is a Senior Principal Consultant and Trainer for the 280 Group. He spent the first twenty years of his career developing software. He has extensive knowledge and experience with the entire software development process ranging from very small to very large projects. During his twelve years writing software at Apple Computer, Jim worked at every level of the operating system. As a member of the QuickTime team, he created the company's innovative audio architecture, earning him two patents and establishing the foundation for countless multimedia products. His contributions include key benefits and innovations found in iTunes and iPod. He was instrumental in designing the user interface and architecture for Kerbango, the world's first stand-alone Internet radio, winning "Best of Show" at the Consumer Electronics Show. Jim served as VP of product management for Meeting Maker, creating the company's product vision and strategy. His accomplishments include expanding into new markets while competing against Microsoft. Jim's efforts revitalized the product through creative repositioning and development of exceptional product benefits. He reorganized the company's product line and extended it by integration and acquisition. Jim has provided product management consulting and training services to a diverse set of Silicon Valley clients ranging from software products to websites. Jim is often described as "visionary." Jim has expertise in product strategy, competitive analysis, market driven requirements, messaging and positioning, and brand building.

Rice, Barbara

Barbara is a Senior Principal Consultant for the 280 Group. She is a marketing professional and strategist, who leads cross-functional, integrated teams for high-tech companies. She specializes in working with companies who need to cost effectively introduce or expand breakout products and programs. She has managed marketing organizations at both large companies and startups, with extensive launch experience and a passion for bringing new products to market.

Rosenfield, Howard

Howard Rosenfield brings over twenty years of experience in venture-backed and public firms. He has held senior marketing, product management, and business development positions at Oracle, Apple, and several venture-backed firms, including Informatica, and NeXT Software. Prior to its acquisition, Howard was vice president of marketing and product management at Blue Titan Software, a venture-backed provider of software for enabling SOA solutions. Over the past decade, Howard has delivered consulting services that helped a variety of small and large organizations build out their product management and marketing operations. Howard earned a BS in Information and Decision Systems from Carnegie Mellon University.

Tan, Adrienne

Adrienne Tan is the Director of brainmates, an Australian product management and marketing agency. She is passionate about helping her clients create products that make a difference in the market. Her time at brainmates has seen her create successful products as diverse as "not for profit" products to an identity theft protection service. Adrienne has twenty years of product management, business improvement, and operational experience in telecommunications and media, having worked for Australia's largest Internet service provider, Telstra BigPond, and AUSTAR, a Cable operator. http://brainmates.com.au

Torres, Dan

Dan Torres is a Silicon Valley native and product management expert who has been delivering products since the days when a 10-megabyte drive had to be shared with a group of eight people (with space to spare) to justify the purchase, to today when building a product launch presentation pushes a gigabyte in size.

Yan-Chatonsky, Natalie

Natalie Yan-Chatonsky is a Product Management Consultant at brainmates and has consulted to clients in a broad range of industries including Cochlear, Telstra Bigpond, AUSTAR and the TV1/SciFi Channels.

Her first degree was a Bachelor of Arts (Asian Studies) at the University of Sydney, Australia, and conducted her final year as a university exchange student at Hosei University, Tokyo, Japan. Prior to consulting at brainmates, she had an extensive career in product management, with technology giants including IBM and Yahoo!. In parallel with her day-job launching digital and mobile products, she went on to broaden her horizons to define and design experiential products and spaces that interact with the five human senses. She carried out her postgraduate studies in Design at the University of Technology and the vocational-based course in Interior Design at the Sydney Institute of Design, TAFE.

She is passionate about product innovation practices and is constantly thinking about how the worlds of design and product management can meet. Read her thoughts on the brainmates blog.
http://brainmates.com.au

Zwinakis, Michaela

Michaela Zwinakis is Vice President of Solution Management, Governance Risk, and Compliance Solutions at SAP in Palo Alto, California. Michaela has been asking "Why?" for over 18 years, working in product management for Symantec, Sun, Sage, Apple, and SAP.

The Product Management Manifesto

I am a Product Management Professional.

I am dedicated to bringing great products to the market. Products that delight my customers. Products that are massively profitable for my company. Products that help change the way people work and live.

In the course of managing my products, there are thousands of small decisions that must be made and tasks that must be accomplished. The sum of these can add up to a phenomenal product. I choose to own the responsibility for making this happen.

I am an expert in all areas regarding my products, customers, the market, technology, competition, channels, press, analysts, trends and anything else that must be taken into account in order to win.

I have a strong vision for my products and develop winning strategies that align with my company's goals and ensure that our investments of time, money, and energy are well spent.

I am committed to using the best methodologies, tools, templates, and techniques available to be more efficient at my job.

I have a plan for my career, and I will further my professional status by attending training courses, becoming certified, and reading books, blogs, and newsletters to learn best practices.

I am the voice of my customers and represent them in every critical decision that is made.

I am a leader. I develop strong alliances with everyone that I need to in order to ensure the success of my product. This includes sales people, engineers, support, customers, channel and business partners, management, the board of directors, and anyone else necessary. Some of these people will be very difficult to work with, but I will find a way to make everyone successful as a team.

I refuse to settle for mediocrity, and I will be tenacious and professional in my approach to getting the best possible results.

I believe that Product Management is one of the toughest, yet more rewarding jobs in the world. Though I will face great odds and challenges, I refuse to become jaded or negative.

Though I have all the responsibility, it is highly likely I have little or no formal authority. Therefore, I will do whatever it takes to persuade others to do what is right for customers and my company.

This manifesto may be downloaded at:
http://www.280group.com/pmmanifesto.pdf.

C Product Management Resources

The 280 Group website is constantly updated with the latest product management and product marketing resources, including:

- Free templates, samples, and white papers
- Product management blogs
- Product management and product marketing books
- Product management associations
- Product management software comparisons
- Product management job listing sites
- 280 LinkedIn Product Management Group (over 18,000 members!)

Visit http://www.280group.com and check the Resources section for the most up-to-date listings. Also, be sure to subscribe to our free *Product Management 2.0* newsletter at http://www.280group.com/newsletters.htm and via RSS to our "Product Management 2.0" Blog located at http://www.280group.com/blog.html.

D Product Management/Marketing Templates

The 280 Group also offers product management and product marketing tool kits, which include templates, narrated training presentations, and samples. The tool kits can be purchased at http://www.280group.com and cover the following topics:

- Product Road Map Toolkit™
- Product Launch Toolkit™
- Product Manager's Toolkit™
- Beta Program Toolkit™
- Product Review Program Toolkit™
- Competitive Analysis Toolkit™
- Developer Program Toolkit™

The 280 Group also makes a number of templates available free for download on the 280 Group website in the Resources section under Free PM Tools, including the following:

- MRD Outline
- Feature Prioritization Matrix
- Beta Program Bug and Feature Database Tools
- AdWords ROI Calculator
- Sample Product Road Maps
- Developer Program Road Map
- Developer Program Cost Estimator Tool
- Evangelism Timeline
- Competitive Feature Matrix Comparison Chart
- Product Launch Marketing Budget
- Product Launch Plan Marketing Budget
- Press Release
- Google AdWords Tips and Strategies

Appendix

E

280 Group Services

The 280 Group helps companies by providing consulting, contractors, training, certification, templates, and books in the areas of product management and product marketing.

If you need assistance with a project or need a professional product management contractor contact us for a free, no-obligation quote.

Our training and certification programs are available as public courses and self-study courses and can be delivered privately onsite for your company. They include the PM Fast Track™, which is designed to turn you into an expert in all areas of the product lifecycle, Agile Product Management Excellence™, the Certified Product Manager™ Self-Study Course & Exam, and the Agile Certified Product Manager™ Self-Study Course and Exam. We also have a wide variety of other courses that can be delivered and range in length from one hour to full days. See our website for additional details.

Appendix

F References

i. Wikipedia contributors, "Henry Ford," *Wikipedia, The Free Encyclopedia,* http://bit.ly/wikiHF[1] (accessed August 24, 2010).

ii. Foust, Dean, "Frederick W. Smith, No Overnight Success," *BusinessWeek,* (Sept 20, 2004), http://bit.ly/BW_FWS.[2]

iii. "FedEx History," http://bit.ly/FedEX.[3]

iv. Wikipedia contributors, "Walkman," *Wikipedia, The Free Encyclopedia,* http://bit.ly/wiki_walkman[4] (accessed August 24, 2010).

v. Wikipedia contributors, "Walkman."

vi. Baba, Marietta L., "Anthropology and Business," in *Encyclopedia of Anthropology,* ed. H. James Birx (Thousand Oaks, CA: Sage Publications, 2006), http://bit.ly/selected_pub.[5]

vii. Baba, 42.

1. en.wikipedia.org/w/index.php?title=Henry_Ford&oldid=378460914
2. www.businessweek.com/magazine/content/04_38/b3900031_mz072.htm
3. about.fedex.designcdt.com/our_company/company_information/fedex_history
4. en.wikipedia.org/w/index.php?title=Walkman&oldid=377559837
5. www.msu.edu/~mbaba/selected_publications.html.

viii. "Ben & Jerry's Mission," http://www.benjerry.com/activism/mission-statement/.

ix. http://www.easyhotel.com/.

x. Brandy N. Frazier, Susan A. Gelman, and Henry M. Wellman, "Preschoolers' Search for Explanatory Information Within Adult-Child Conversation," *Child Development* 80 (2009): 1592–1611.

About the Authors

Brian Lawley is the CEO and founder of the 280 Group (http://www.280group.com), which provides product management consulting, contractors, training and templates. During the last twenty-five years of his career he has shipped more than fifty successful products. He is the former President of the Silicon Valley Product Management Association, won the 2008 AIPMM award for Excellence in Thought Leadership for Product Management, and is the author of the best-selling books *Expert Product Management* and *The Phenomenal Product Manager*. Mr. Lawley has been featured on CNBC's World Business Review and the Silicon Valley Business Report and writes articles for a variety of publications including the *Product Management 2.0* newsletter and blog. Mr. Lawley holds a BS in Management Science with a minor in Music Technology from the University of California, San Diego and an MBA with honors from San Jose State University.

Greg Cohen is a Senior Principal Consultant with the 280 Group and a fifteen-year product management veteran with extensive experience and knowledge of Agile development, a Certified Scrum Master, and former President of the Silicon Valley Product Management Association. He has worked and consulted to venture start-ups and large companies alike and has trained product managers throughout the world on Agile development, road mapping, feature prioritization, product lifecycle process, and product management assessment. Greg is the author of the book *Agile Excellence for Product Managers* and a speaker and frequent commentator on product management issues.

Greg has a background in B2B software and Software-as-a-Service (SaaS) including spend analysis, business analytics, contract management, network security, and medical technology. Prior to consulting, he has managed over a dozen products from concept through deployment and end-of-life for Silicon Valley companies such as Instill (acquired by iTradeNetworks,) Idealab!, and Pandesic (a joint venture between Intel and SAP).

Greg earned an MBA with honors from Babson College and a BS in Mechanical Engineering with a second major in Electrical Engineering from Tufts University.

Write Your Own Rules

You can write your own 42 Rules book, and we can help you do it—from initial concept, to writing and editing, to publishing and marketing. If you have a great idea for a 42 Rules book, then we want to hear from you.

As you know, the books in the 42 Rules series are practical guidebooks that focus on a single topic. The books are written in an easy-to-read format that condenses the fundamental elements of the topic into 42 Rules. They use realistic examples to make their point and are fun to read.

Two Kinds of 42 Rules Books

42 Rules books are published in two formats: the single-author book and the contributed-author book. The single-author book is a traditional book written by one author. The contributed-author book (like *42 Rules of Product Management*) is a compilation of Rules, each written by a different contributor, which support the main topic. If you want to be the sole author of a book or one of its contributors, we can help you succeed!

42 Rules Program

A lot of people would like to write a book, but only a few actually do. Finding a publisher, and distributing and marketing the book are challenges that prevent even the most ambitious of authors to ever get started.

At 42 Rules, we help you focus on and be successful in the writing of your book. Our program concentrates on the following tasks so you don't have to.

- **Publishing:** You receive expert advice and guidance from the Executive Editor, copy editors, technical editors, and cover and layout designers to help you create your book.
- **Distribution:** We distribute your book through the major book distribution channels, like Baker & Taylor and Ingram, Amazon.com, Barnes and Noble, Borders Books, etc.
- **Marketing:** 42 Rules has a full-service marketing program that includes a customized Web page for you and your book, email registrations and campaigns, blogs, webcasts, media kits and more.

Whether you are writing a single-authored book or a contributed-author book, you will receive editorial support from 42 Rules Executive Editor, Laura Lowell, author of '42 Rules of Marketing,' which was rated Top 5 in Business Humor and Top 25 in Business Marketing on Amazon.com (December 2007), and author and Executive Editor of '42 Rules for Working Moms.'

Accepting Submissions

If you want to be a successful author, we'll provide you the tools to help make it happen. Start today by answering the following questions and visit our website at http://superstarpress.com/ for more information on submitting your 42 Rules book idea.

Super Star Press is now accepting submissions for books in the 42 Rules book series. For more information, email info@superstarpress.com or call 408-257-3000.

Other Happy About Books

Expert Product Management

This book teaches both new and seasoned Product Managers and Product Marketers powerful and effective ways to ensure they give their products the best possible chance for success.

Paperback: $19.95
eBook: $14.95

The Phenomenal Product Manager

This book goes beyond the basics and teaches you how to work more effectively with your teams, how to influence when you have no formal authority, how to get the most important work done in less time and how to manage and accelerate your career.

Paperback: $19.95
eBook: $14.95

Agile Excellence for Product Managers

Agile Excellence for Product Managers is a plain speaking guide on how to work with Agile development teams to achieve phenomenal product success.

Paperback: $24.95
eBook: $14.95

Get Out of the Way

This book offers strategies for empowering, encouraging, and directing a top-notch development team. This book is a must have for all managers of engineering, software-development, IT, and other high-tech development organizations, as well as the executives who do business with them.

Paperback: $19.95
eBook: $14.95

Purchase these books at Happy About
http://happyabout.info/
or at other online and physical bookstores.

A Message From Super Star Press™

Thank you for your purchase of this 42 Rules Series book. It is available online at:
http://www.happyabout.com/42rules/42rulesproductmanagement.php
or at other online and physical bookstores. To learn more about contributing to books in the 42 Rules series, check out http://superstarpress.com.

Please contact us for quantity discounts at sales@superstarpress.com.

If you want to be informed by email of upcoming books, please email bookupdate@superstarpress.com.

CPSIA information can be obtained at www.ICGtesting.com
Printed in the USA
LVOW091320070812

293288LV00005B/30/P